Enjoying
GOD

LLOYD OGILVIE

WORD PUBLISHING
Dallas · London · Sydney · Singapore

ENJOYING GOD

Copyright © 1989 by Lloyd Ogilvie. All rights reserved. No portion of this
book may be reproduced in any form, except for brief quotations in reviews,
without written permission from the publisher.

All Scripture quotations, unless otherwise noted, are from The Holy Bible,
New King James Version, copyright © 1979, 1980, 1982 by Thomas Nelson,
Inc. Used by permission.

Library of Congress Cataloging-in-Publication Data

Ogilvie, Lloyd John.
    Enjoying God / Lloyd Ogilvie.
      p.   cm.
    ISBN 0-8499-0521-4
    1. Joy—Biblical teaching.   2. Bible. N.T. Ephesians—Criticism,
interpretation, etc.   I. Title.
    BS2655.J6045   1989
    248.4—dc20   89-39220
                                                             CIP

9 8 0 1 2 3 9   MP   9 8 7 6 5 4 3 2 1

Printed in the United States of America

CONTENTS

To
James Shuemaker
friend, encourager, and
fellow adventurer in the Kingdom

ACKNOWLEDGMENTS

You will note that I have not written a long introduction to this book. For good reason. Frankly, I'm so enthused about what I want to share about enjoying God that I want to move directly to the first chapter.

But first I want to express my deep appreciation for the people who have helped make this book possible.

I want to thank my assistant, Stewart McLaurin, for overseeing the total project and for all he does to effectively facilitate the aspects of my professional life.

My new friend, Rick Nau, transcribed and edited a series of sermons on Ephesians I did some time ago, These transcripts provided me with a starting point as I wrote several of the chapters in this book. Rick's enthusiasm for the project was a great encouragement to me. I'm thankful for his willingness to invest his professional skills in this aspect of the ministry of our church. I also appreciate the continued help of our church librarian, William McCalmont, who does weekly research to help me in my sermon preparations.

The major responsibility for putting this book together was assumed by June Mears, my publications assistant. She processed the manuscript through several revisions and did the creative editing of the manuscript. I appreciate all she has done to help me express more clearly what I want to communicate in this book. And gratitude is expressed to Susan Roberto for her assistance and to Sue Muhler for her proofreading and editing.

Of course, no manuscript is finished when it leaves the author's hands. My friends at Word, Inc., have been wonderful teammates in the ministry of communication.

I want to express my thanks to my friend of many years, Al Bryant, managing editor of trade publications, for his careful editing and preparation of the final manuscript for publication.

Charles "Kip" Jordon, senior vice-president and publisher of Word, Inc., is a publisher with a mission, who has been consistently focused on his vision for communicating through the written word. His clear purpose of proclaiming Christ, serving the church, and reaching the secular American has been both liberating and inspiring to me as a writer. I'm indebted to him for his friendship and for making working with Word, Inc., like being part of a family.

Throughout the preparation of this book and over the years, Ernest Owen, senior vice-president of acquisitions, has been a close personal friend and prayer partner. My life has been deeply enriched by his friendship.

To all of these friends and creative professionals I express my profound gratitude.

Lloyd Ogilvie

Enjoying

GOD

1

ENJOYING
GOD

"Who do you want to be for your children?" This was the question
I asked a group of fathers at a men's retreat. I also asked them what
they wanted to receive from their children. Some fathers wanted
to be a good example for their children and desired obedience
from them. Others wanted to be good providers for their families
and wanted their children's appreciation.

But I liked one man's answer: "I just want to be the kind of
person my children really enjoy and I want them to know how
much I enjoy them!"

Multiply that father's desire a billion times and we have a
faint glimpse of God's longing toward us. It's an awesome thought
to realize that God enjoys us and wants us to enjoy Him. His love
for us encompasses and exceeds a father's and mother's delight in
a newborn child.

You and I were created to enjoy God.

Enjoy God? Isn't the word "enjoy" a bit frivolous to describe
our relationship with Almighty God?

Not when we understand the deeper meaning of enjoyment.
Authentic enjoyment is the experience and expression of joy.

And true joy is the outward manifestation of the inner grip of grace on our souls.

So, enjoying God begins with the sheer delight of knowing God and receiving His unmerited favor and unqualified love. We rejoice with unrestrained praise for who God is as our Father; we respond to Him with uncontainable adoration for all He has done, is doing, and will continue to do for us in and through Jesus Christ; and we receive with unlimited gratitude His gift of power, guidance, wisdom and hope through His indwelling Spirit.

At the time I'm writing this, my newest granddaughter, Bonnie Ghlee Ogilvie, is six months old. One day my wife Mary Jane and I had the privilege of baby-sitting her. I eagerly came home to enjoy being with my granddaughter. When Bonnie saw me, she squirmed with recognition and reached out her arms to be held.

"Mary Jane!" I exclaimed with delight. "Bonnie recognizes me and wants to be held!"

And, oh, how I enjoyed cuddling that lovely little lass!

Do we dare to assume that God longs for the same response from us throughout our lives? Is that too sentimental? Or, is it too exalted?

A lad said to his dad, "Papa, you're great! I just want to be with you!"

I felt the same thing at dawn today about my heavenly Father as I began my morning devotions.

One of the most liberating discoveries of my life is that I was born and reborn to enjoy God and know the inexplicable delight of His enjoying me. Of course, I've known His judgment as a part of His gracious care. He is continually calling me toward His best for my life. He offers me limitless encouragement to press on in the quest to do His will. What a dynamic motivation it is to know that I can bring joy—the essence of enjoyment— to Him!

THE DELIGHT OF GOD

And He has clearly told us what delights Him most. "Let him who glories glory in this, that he understands and knows Me, that I am the Lord, exercising lovingkindness, judgment, and righteousness in the earth. For in these I delight" (Jer. 9:24).

The secret of enjoying God is discovering that what provides Him with enjoyment in us is also what produces lasting enjoyment for us. There's no greater enjoyment in life than bringing delight to our Father. And His delight is that we understand and know Him.

But God does not leave us wandering in a spiritual desert in search of the authentic enjoyment of knowing Him. The astounding truth is that He inspires in us what He desires from us. He is both the initiator and instigator of the mutual enjoyment He wants us to experience in our relationship with Him.

God has written His signature in the natural world and has given us the capacity to recognize and appreciate the splendid beauty. He has blessed us with an abundance of natural resources to relish with grateful reverence. He has entrusted to us loved ones and friends to share the pleasures of life. With providential care, He has arranged circumstances of our lives for our ultimate good and has given us strength to live at full potential. And His admonition is: "Enjoy!"

But there's more. Much more. So that we might know Him personally, He has come in Jesus Christ to reveal His true nature. In Christ we experience His lovingkindness, judgment, and righteousness. We have been loved to the uttermost, forgiven, and made right with Him through the cross. Now God's admonition is: "Enjoy all I've done for you!"

But press on. God gently creates in us a desire to know Him. He gives us the gift of faith to accept His love. He woos us to Him. Our experience teaches us that His promises are true. He will never leave us nor forsake us. Our knowledge of Him grows. At first, the awesome truths about God and His nature seemed beyond us, almost incomprehensible. We felt awe and wonder, but little joy. But then, as we come to know the Father personally in the intimacy of prayer, we grow in the assurance that He will never let us down. He gives us strength when we are weak, gracious correction when we fail, and undeserved grace when we sin. He lifts us up when we fall and gives us new beginnings when we were devoid of hope. And just when we think there was no way out of a difficulty, He opened a door of opportunity. *Now* God's admonition is: "Enjoy your Father Who loves you!"

3

Then it happens. We begin the wondrous experience of enjoying God for Himself without becoming irreverent. We say with Joyce Kilmer, "And thank God for God!" Who God is in His love, mercy, and bracing encouragement becomes more important than anything He can give to us. Our growing relationship with God Himself becomes the source of our holy enjoyment of Him. Then our enjoyment of all He does and provides for us is maximized. And God is delighted.

Enjoyment, The Ultimate Stage

I'm convinced that enjoyment is the ultimate stage of knowledge. When we set out to learn the basic truths of an intellectual discipline, we are confounded by all we don't know. Little by little, we become more secure in ideas and theories. Then one day, we suddenly realize that we have captured the subject and know how to use our knowledge. What was previously frustrating becomes enjoyable.

As a young doctor put it, "Lloyd, I'm finally enjoying the practice of medicine. All the years of education and internship are paying off. Now it's a joy to be a doctor!"

The same is true in learning a sport. A championship golfer told me, "I used to hate golf. I was never sure I could hit the ball straight or far. It was so frustrating! Then, eventually, I got my swing grooved and my rhythm in sync. Soon it became fun. Now I'd rather play golf than eat!" The woman had been trying to get into golf. And suddenly, golf had gotten into her.

More profoundly, enjoyment of our faith grows in the same way. In the beginning, God seems distant and aloof. Biblical and theological terms are like a foreign language. Our prayers are strained and shallow. We try hard to be faithful and consistent disciples. And then, with the touch of the Father's hand, we discover how much He loves us and wants us to know Him personally. Secondary theories about Him are replaced by an intimate relationship with Him. None of our awe and adoration is lost as we begin to enjoy Him. Enjoying God is not an immature step of growth but the sublime stage of knowing Him. To really know Him is to enjoy Him.

ENJOYING GOD IS GLORIFYING GOD

The authors of the Westminster Shorter Catechism were also convinced about the powerful relationship of both knowing and enjoying God. They firmly believed in the sovereignty of God. For them, God was in charge of history and the life of the individual. In 1647 they wrote their stirring thoughts about the majesty of God in the catechism and asked: "What is man's chief end?" And they answered, "To glorify God and enjoy Him forever."

Enjoying God is really a vital expression of glorifying Him. The glory of God is the manifestation and revelation of all that He is as Creator, Sustainer, Redeemer, and Lord of all. We glorify Him when we worship Him for His lovingkindness, goodness, and mercifulness. Our worship becomes intimate when we joyfully experience God's nature and attributes. From that joy springs our desire to glorify Him by serving Him. Our faithful obedience becomes an enjoyable response.

And God enjoys us. Have you ever thought of God *enjoying* you? That may be a shocking thought to you! Immediately we think of all the reasons why God couldn't possibly enjoy us. We make a mental checklist of all the things we do and say that should displease God. Certainly, He does not enjoy our failures and problems, or our resistance to His guidance. Nor does He delight in the pain and suffering we bring upon ourselves and onto others. But He does delight in us as persons.

God's enjoyment of us is never conditional as ours is with each other. He created us for a relationship with Himself and is continually working to convince us of how precious we are to Him so that we might enjoy Him. He knows that if we deeply believed that He enjoys us, we'd spend our lives bringing joy to Him by enjoying our status as His cherished people.

TRULY ENJOYING LIFE

This book is about learning the secret to the lost art of truly enjoying life. It's written for people who struggle. For many years I have collected the repeated responses to surveys about the struggles we face in living life to the fullest. I am convinced that the single most painful struggle we share is the difficulty of entrusting God with our struggles!

We live impoverished lives spiritually because we don't know how spiritually rich we are. Life's struggles defeat us because we forget the limitless inheritance from our Father to enjoy.

We are like a person who thinks he does not have adequate financial resources to meet his daily needs. When he is told that he has received a great inheritance, he is astounded, but lifelong patterns keep him from using the inheritance freely.

Hetty Green was like that. When Hetty died she left an estate valued at more than one hundred million dollars. Hetty denied herself any pleasures. She did not use any of her wealth to live comfortably or to care for the needs of others. Her life was a constant struggle. She ate cold oatmeal to save on cooking fuel. Hetty never heated her house. When her son needed medical attention for a growth on his leg, she hesitated calling a doctor and instead searched for a free clinic. She stalled so long that her son's leg had to be amputated. Hetty lived as a pauper when, in fact, she was wealthy.

That's a shocking story. But it's no more shocking than those of us who live as spiritual paupers. We live with a lid on our expectations of what God is able to do to help us. Reservations, caution, fear, and worry dominate our lives. We need to review our spiritual wealth and then learn to draw on what God has put at our disposal.

THE BIBLICAL FOUNDATION TO ENJOYING GOD

Around A.D. 62, the apostle Paul wrote a magnificent description of our inheritance in an epistle to the Christians in Roman Asia Minor. It's called Ephesians. The letter was circulated among the churches of the province and later became identified with the most prominent church in Ephesus. The words, "in Ephesus" do not appear in the earliest manuscripts and most scholars agree that it was a circulated letter. It was not written to confront problems in any one church but to help all the Christians in the area to claim their spiritual riches. The epistle is a stunning, comprehensive review of the grace of God, His mighty acts in Christ, and His presence with us, as well as a review on how we are to live as His people, His Church.

Ephesians is the solid biblical foundation of this book on enjoying God, and plumbing its depths is exactly what we will do as we move through its promises and assurances.

In soaring rhetoric Paul gives us the source of our joy. He explains the basics of our adoption, eternal security, the cross, redemption, and the infilling of the Spirit. Paul's focus is on the reigning Christ and repeats the theme through the phrase: "In Christ."

The first three chapters deal with our eternal position in Christ, while the last three chapters examine the practice of the Christian life. More than any other book in the New Testament, Ephesians helps us enjoy God, all that He had done for us, and the exciting things we can dare to attempt by His power.

Moving through Ephesians in the context of learning to enjoy God is like hearing the reading of a will in which we are named beneficiaries. Just when we are about to settle for a grim life of struggling on our own, we are told about the "exceeding riches" that are ours. The multi-faceted splendor of these spiritual riches prompt us to ask, "Why am I living a frustrating life of struggle when all this grace is offered to me?"

But we will press on beyond the "why" of that question to the "how" of grace-motivated, grace-empowered, grace-communicated living.

The title of this book came from an expression a woman used while explaining to the elders of my church what she and her husband discovered through an exciting renewal of their faith. You'll appreciate what she said when you learn a bit of her spiritual journey. Your story may be like hers. Or your struggle may be very different. But we all long to move beyond struggling to the bliss of enjoying God.

RELIGION WITHOUT JOY

Lucille was raised in a strict religious family. During her teenage years in a rules-oriented church, she learned a great deal about God's judgment, but little of the joy of knowing Him. After attending an equally joyless church college, Lucille moved to Los Angeles where she met and married Dan, who had a similar religious upbringing. Together they found a church that emulated their background and became active members for more than ten years. Each week they were reminded of how sinful they were, but were never taught how great God is. They felt empty. Eventually they stopped attending church services. Prayer became a drudgery and soon became sporadic. Meanwhile, they became engrossed in the demands of Dan's career, building a home, and raising a family. But they felt a lingering uneasiness.

About that time, Lucille met Sally, one of the most contagious Christians in my church. Sally sparkles with radiant joy. She invited Lucille and Dan to visit our church during a time when I was preaching a series on the grace of God from Ephesians. Lucille and Dan returned for the weekly messages. Each week I gave an invitation at the conclusion of the service for people to come forward to the chancel to pray with the pastors and elders of the church.

One Sunday, it was my privilege to pray with Lucille and Dan. They asked to receive grace to fill their emptiness. And during the prayer they experienced a profound assurance that they were loved and cherished by God.

That was only the beginning. Lucille and Dan became part of a small group of spiritual adventurers who meet weekly to study the Bible, share needs, and pray for one another. Affirmation and encouragement flowed freely for Lucille and Dan and they were set free of their dread of God and came to know and love Him as their gracious Father.

When they met with the elders in preparation for uniting with the church, Lucille said something I'll never forget. As I mentioned, what she said gave me the idea for the title of this book.

"There are no other words to express how I feel than to say that in the past year *Dan and I have come to enjoy God.* I hope you won't think that's flippant. But for years we've lived in a kind of dread of never measuring up, of always feeling we had to be better for God to love us. Strange as it may seem, we've been Christians most of our lives, but never really experienced His grace. Ever since we received His grace one Sunday in worship, we've not stopped growing in the sheer wonder of His goodness. Now it's a joy to serve Him!"

My prayer is that this will be your experience as we enjoy God and the riches of His grace in these following chapters. Together we're going to glorify God *and* enjoy Him!

WHAT
A
SAINT
YOU
ARE

You are special!

Our first step in enjoying God is to delight in being chosen and cherished. It's claiming that we are saints.

Paul simply addressed his letter to the first-century Christians with, "To the saints." The distortions of the term "saints" through the centuries makes it difficult for us to appreciate what it means to be a saint.

For some, the word "saint" is a term of endearment. One evening, my wife and I were having dinner in a lovely, candlelit restaurant. We couldn't help overhearing the conversation of a couple seated nearby. At the end of the evening, the woman reached across the table, took her husband's hand and said, "Oh, what a saint you are for giving me this evening out!" The man may have been a saint in the true sense, but taking his wife out for dinner didn't make him so!

Others use the term "saint" to identify a superlative charac-ter. "Now there's a real saint," we say when we want to recognize superior spirituality. We imply that not every Christian *is* a saint. But according to Paul, true sainthood is not achieved by our

perfection or the impeccability of our piety or our achievements in Christian service.

Evidence of the misuse of the word is best seen in how few Christians feel comfortable being called saints. For example, once I addressed a group of Presbyterian church elders by saying, "Good evening, saints!"

My greeting was received by uneasy titters and surprised glances. One man shouted from the audience, "They haven't arrived yet!"

But they had. The elders were unaware that they were the saints.

We usually think of saints as characters portrayed in stained glass windows or as heroes and heroines described on the pages of history. In Ambrose Bierce's *The Devil's Dictionary*, a saint is defined as "a dead sinner, revised and edited."

But what about living saints who are redeemed and edified?

Our eagerness to claim our sainthood is further dulled by the practice of canonizing deceased Christians to "sainthood." The Vatican has a special committee responsible for scrutinizing candidates. According to my understanding of the qualifications for sainthood, a potential saint must have had a vision of Christ, performed at least two miracles, exemplified superior piety, and mediated healings after his or her death. All the evidence from the person's lifetime and all contemporary claims of miracles are carefully researched and authenticated by this committee.

You might think I'm coat-tailing it when I tell you that Rome recently elevated John Ogilvie to sainthood. He's now known as "Saint John Ogilvie." I mentioned part of the story in a previous book, but now there's more to tell.

John Ogilvie was the last of Scotland's martyrs. He defected from his Calvinistic upbringing, moved to France, and became a Jesuit priest. Later, he returned to Scotland. Because of his Roman Catholicism and his political opposition to the crown, he was hanged in the city square in Glasgow. What a pity! John Ogilvie was a loyal, gracious servant of Christ.

Years after his death, people began using medallions bearing his image during prayer. Apparently these medallions have been effective in miraculous healings for more than four centuries.

In this past decade, several healings assured his elevation to sainthood. For example, in Scotland there is a man by the name of John Fagin who held the medallion of Blessed John Ogilvie in his hand as he prayed and was healed of what had been diagnosed as incurable cancer.

I believe another kind of healing occurred in Blessed John Ogilvie's name during the elevation ceremonies in Rome. The pope invited the moderator of the Church of Scotland to participate in the ceremonies, expressing a spirit of ecumenism and a healing of wounds between the two denominations.

When I was in Scotland recently, a man in the Highlands remarked, "Ach, I see one of your clan made it to sainthood."

A friend who overheard the tongue-in-cheek comment said, "And so have you, Lloyd. You'll never be more of a saint than you are now."

The same is true for you if you have accepted the biblical qualifications of sainthood.

My purpose here is not to enter into a polemic about the practice of elevating historic persons to sainthood or about praying in their name, but simply to underline the confusion caused in so many people's minds about their own status as saints today.

Among the laity, Protestants generally think of saints as super-Christians. Roman Catholics consider them to be those now in heaven who were used mightily on earth. Many people in both groups want to enjoy their spiritual status now, but don't know how to do it. I want to help us all claim our current spiritual status.

The term "saint" is used sixty-two times in the Bible to describe the position of believers. Nowhere is sainthood associated with performance. An exposition of the first verse of Ephesians gives us the four dynamics of enjoying our sainthood: "Paul, an apostle of Jesus Christ by the will of God, to the saints who are in Ephesus, and faithful in Christ Jesus."

Let's break the verse down and savor its nourishment for our hungry hearts.

SAINTS ARE SINGULARLY SELECTED

Paul declares that he was an apostle of Jesus Christ, by the will of God. Here the word "will" comes from the Greek word *thelema*

rather than *boulema*. *Thelema* means the desire of God which, to be fully appropriated, requires the cooperation of the human spirit. *Boulema* is the immutable, irrevocable will of God. It will be accomplished whether or not we cooperate.

God exercised His *boulema* will when He came in Jesus Christ to reconcile the world to Himself. "God was in Christ reconciling the world" (2 Cor. 5:19). This verse describes the center of Christianity. God couldn't be stopped. Our sovereign God acted to accomplish His benevolent purpose out of sheer grace. In Jesus Christ, the God-man, God revealed who He is and who we were meant to be. Jesus' central message was the kingdom of God: His rule and reign in us, between us and others, and in all of life. The Messiah went to the cross by the irrevocable will of God. "Him, being delivered by the determined counsel and foreknowledge of God" (Acts 2:23). The Greek word for counsel also comes from *boulema*. No human effort could have stopped the cross.

On Calvary the atoning heart of the Father was revealed and fulfilled. Christ died for us in a once-never-to-be-repeated atonement to forgive our sins and make us right with God. God exonerated us. He set us free of guilt and condemnation.

By His same immutable will, God, whose Father-heart pulsated in indefatigable love on the cross, raised Christ from the dead. He made the resurrected Christ the reigning Lord, Emmanuel, God with us forever.

To be "in Christ" is to be a recipient of all that God has done for us through the atonement and to be in a personal relationship with the present reigning Savior. Christ takes up residence in us as indwelling Lord. We become His postresurrection home!

But we are not His home without our willingness. This is where the *thelema* will of God enters.

Paul became an apostle by the *thelema* of God. He was elected, called, set apart, and chosen by the desire of God. Yet Paul was not a puppet on a string. He could have resisted his call. But, through Christ, Paul was given the ability to choose to be chosen.

What does this mean for our sainthood? Everything! By the irrevocable will of God, our salvation has been accomplished. By

12

His gracious choice we have been called to accept salvation. The first thing we claim, then, is that we are saints by God's choice. But what are we chosen to do?

A SAINT IS HOLY

We are chosen to be holy. This is what the word "saint" means. In Greek, the word is *hagios,* meaning holy, set apart, and belonging to God. It does not mean the spiritual elitism of a "Holy Joe" or the aloof smugness of a "Perfect Pat." Rather, it indicates ownership. God says to us, "You belong to Me!"

When Paul addressed the saints, he was not writing to church leaders or to spiritually advanced people. Rather, Paul wrote to all of God's people who stood equally with him as those chosen, called, and cherished.

We, then, can also enjoy our status as loved and forgiven people.

This is a lofty thought, but what does it mean practically? Nothing less than that all we are and have belongs to God. This means our minds, emotions, will and bodies belong to God. We expand God's reign in our lives to include the people, the possessions, and the plans of our lives. And we don't stop here. Our list grows to include the memories that shape our present and the values that etch our future. In addition, we must be sure to include our work world where we spend most of our days. We must also remember that our money is holy, too.

Choosing to be chosen means accepting Christ's lordship over our total lives. This requires our committed surrender to Him.

A SAINT IS FAITHFUL

Paul continues: "To the saints who are in Ephesus, and faithful in Christ Jesus."

Saints are not only selected and belong to God, but they are faithful. The adjective faithful, in Greek *pistos,* can mean either "having faith" or "being faithful." I think Paul intended both usages. A saint, really, is one who both receives and exercises faith. Faith is a gift of the Spirit given to us to respond to the gospel. Our primary faith grows and is expressed in moment-by-moment trust. Then we develop a consistent faithfulness that is essential to the character of a saint. Our only concern is to discover what the Lord wants us to do and to do it with joy.

The dynamic growth of faith is expressed by Paul in Rom. 1:16–17: "For I am not ashamed of the gospel of Christ, for it is the power of God to salvation for everyone who believes, for the Jew first and also for the Greek. For in it the righteousness of God is revealed from faith to faith; as it is written, 'The just shall live by faith.'"

The phrase "by faith" communicates the open secret of enjoying God. There is no other way to please Him or experience His pleasure in us.

By faith we accept His call; by faith we receive His grace in Christ; by faith we know we are forgiven; by faith we open our minds and hearts to His indwelling power. Then each day, through our faithfulness, we commit our challenges and opportunities to Him. We trust that He will work in us and in our circumstances to accomplish His purposes and to draw us closer in an intimate relationship with Him. Living by faith is exciting!

A SAINT IS ORDINARY

This may surprise you after all the grand things I've said about our awesome status as saints. By saying a saint is ordinary, I mean that he or she lives in sainthood through the common, everyday routines of life.

Paul wrote his letter to the saints in Ephesus and throughout Asia Minor. It was in those pagan cities that their sainthood clashed with secularism. Ephesus was the "Vanity Fair" of the area, with the cult of Diana dominating the city. It was a sensual, sex-centric, materialistic center of humanism.

Throughout the other cities of the province, temples were being built for the imperial cult of Caesar worship. In some cities, a person could not be employed without belonging to a trade guild. But a certificate from the imperial cult was required for the document. To get this, one had to enter the temple, take a pinch of incense and say, "Caesar is Lord." Many of Paul's fellow Christians were unemployed because they could not comply.

The pagan cults were not the only problem. Christian heresies created by the syncretistic mixing of religions were springing up everywhere. Some heresies were a subtle blend of philosophical ideas and Christianity. The Essenes espoused legalism while the Gnostics championed an esoteric knowledge of God. Jesus was considered only one of the angelic emanations from God and not the preexistent Christ, Redeemer, and only Savior. The Christians were constantly confronted with the practices of eccentric cults that served up a nauseating brew of Christian beliefs and lawless behavior. All we need to do is read the letters of the risen Christ in Revelation 2 and 3 to understand the difficulties the saints faced in Asia Minor. Much of what He condemned in those cities had begun or was in full swing when Paul wrote Ephesians. In the midst of ordinary life in Asia Minor the Christians had to live out their faith.

How could anyone enjoy being a saint under these conditions? Only because the believers were able to fully experience their riches in Christ was life in Ephesus or anywhere else endurable.

The Christians defined and described enjoyment with a word different from that of the Greeks. The Greek word for enjoyment is *hedone,* from which we derive "hedonism," the gratification of our desires without restraint. The Christians employed another word, *apolausis,* which Paul used in his first letter to Timothy in Ephesus to remind him that "the living God gives us richly all things to *enjoy*" (1 Tim. 6:17).

We find pleasure in discovering and doing His will that satisfies the deepest longing of our hearts and redirects our energies to serving others, rather than using them.

Christ in us gives us courage to take a stand for what we believe and to endure when we are tempted to yield to pressures, to conform, and to be captured by our culture.

I would not have wanted to have been in Ephesus, Smyrna, Pergamos, Thyatira, Sardis, Philadelphia, or Laodicea without also being in Christ and having Him live in me. Nor would I want to be in Los Angeles, London, Johannesburg, or Crossbow, Wyoming, without the power of Christ. When we enjoy His presence anywhere, we can focus on serving Him and others. Because we are in His presence we don't need ultimate security in any given place.

Do I really mean this? I want to. As with you, secondary things are always competing for first place in my life. I like my job, appreciate my house, and am happily settled in Los Angeles. In all these places, I'm called to live out my sainthood. Enjoying my sainthood frees me to enjoy the gifts the Lord provides without making any one of them the primary source of my enjoyment. This is reserved for Him. We are to *enjoy* God and *use* things. Never turn this around!

The best correction to remember is that we've been called into sainthood to serve. To be in Christ is to be in ministry. People become the primary focus. The more we enjoy being saints, the more the Lord's love, forgiveness and sacrificial caring surge through us to others. Serving people is also the most creative motive for confronting and seeking to change the social problems and needs which others face. In this, a saint is fearless!

WHO ARE YOU?

Some time ago I attended a meeting of leaders who knew each other by profession or accomplishment, but not as persons. Before we began the meeting, the leader wisely asked us to introduce ourselves with a word or a phrase. We could not say anything that might identify what we do. We had to use language that exposed who we are. What a challenge that was for most of the people whose activities and positions are the essential meaning of their lives.

How would you have answered? What's the one word that expresses the essence of you? Would it embarrass you if I said, "I'm Saint Lloyd John Ogilvie by the grace of God?" If so, you still may be laboring with some limited ideas about sainthood. I suggest you take the lid off your reservations. Accept your status. You belong to God. Calvary was for you as if you'd been the only person alive that Friday. And Pentecost was for you as if you'd been the only one in the Upper Room. The gift of faith is offered freely to you. His gift liberates you to pray, "Lord, I believe in you and commit my life to You."

When you pray this prayer, a conviction will grow inside you. In boldness you will think: "Jesus is Lord! He is My Lord! I will live the rest of my life for His glory!"

Your sainthood is settled: Your status is secure. It's part of our inheritance. *Enjoy!*

YOU
ARE
LOVED
NOW!

There are four words we all need to hear more than any other four words in all the world.

I know I need to hear them. And years of feeling the pulse of people's hurts and hopes convinces me that you need to hear them. Hourly. Daily. Right now.

We wistfully long to hear these four words from one another. Our deepest yearning is to hear them from the Lord.

What are these four powerful, healing, liberating words?

Listen, listen to the whisper of the Lord in your soul.

You are loved now!

Did you hear the whisper?

Those words are the essence of grace and grace's heart companion, peace.

Recently I asked people to send me their most urgent questions. Questions of all kinds came pouring in, filling the mailbags. Some people asked personal questions about life, others asked theological questions about God and His will, while a few asked biblical questions about difficult passages. One person simply sent

17

in a postcard with this question scrawled across the back, "Is there any word from the Lord?" We all ask this question.

The word He whispers is grace. We should not be surprised by His whisper because He *is* grace. He also is mercy, everlasting compassion, and healing love. Lovingkindness filled the Father's heart for His estranged people until at last His heart overflowed in the gift of His Son.

Grace is the love that Christ defined. He incarnated it, revealed it, communicated it, and went to the cross to redeem us so we could experience it. Now Christ is the grace of God with us.

He whispers in our souls,

"You are loved now!"

Did you hear Him?

"Grace to you and peace from God our Father and the Lord Jesus Christ," Paul wrote at the opening of Ephesians. Paul's greeting was more than a traditional one. Rather, it pulsated with the drum-beat rhythms in his heart and expressed the commanding conviction of his mind. The greeting is really the apostle's topic sentence for all he wanted to write, a concise summary of his whole letter. "Grace and peace to you!" We will hear this triumphant theme throughout our review of our spiritual inheritance recorded so eloquently in Ephesians.

Thus far we have established that we were created to accept our inheritance and enjoy God who gives it to us freely and lavishly. We also affirmed that our privilege to draw on this inheritance is our "rebirth" right as saints. But we need to be careful that the opening words of the reading of the will won't be dulled by our faithless familiarity or blocked by our self-negation.

Did you hear the whisper?

"You are loved now!"

HARD OF HEARING

Many of us are hard of hearing when it comes to hearing His whisper of grace and receiving the peace it should provide. These four words—"You are loved now!"—may be difficult for many of us to accept or appropriate because of the conditioning of our past. The words turn our view of ourselves upside down. Often we negate them because we have been taught to be our own stern judge and therefore cannot hear them.

The words "you are loved" are difficult enough, but when you add "now," we're unsettled. *Now* may be too soon for stingy receivers.

Someday, maybe, we think. *Sometime when we get our act together, shape up our personalities and get rid of our bad habits or wandering nonpublic thoughts and fantasies—then, perhaps then. But certainly not now.*

Or, God's whisper may be difficult to hear for us because we are so full of memories of things said or done in the past. We feel alarmed rather than assured. We think, *Hold on a minute. If you knew about me you wouldn't say that. Surely there's something I must do to earn that kind of grace, like make amends, work out my guilt, or perform some kind of penance.* So we push away God's unmerited favor, thinking we can balance the scales of our failures.

MET AT THE PASS

A man who attended worship at my church for several months came to see me. He's an outstanding and successful business leader who appears secure. He said, "Lloyd, you talk so often about God's unqualified love. But I want to introduce you to a person who makes it very difficult to accept that. He meets me at the pass and says, 'John, you have no right to accept that. You're not worthy. Someday, but not yet!' That person lives inside my own skin."

QUID PRO QUO CONDITIONING

I empathized with John. My own formative years had ingrained the quid pro quo into my attitude toward myself: *do and you'll receive; perform and you'll be loved.* When I got good grades, achieved, and was a success, I felt acceptance from my parents. My dad taught me to fish and hunt and worked hard to provide for us, but I rarely heard him say, "Lloyd, I love you." He tried to show it in actions, and sometimes I caught a twinkle of affirmation in his eyes. But I still felt empty.

When I became a Christian, I immediately became so involved in discipleship activities that I did not experience the

19

Reflecting on that day, Allistair told me, "It was grace that did it. I could have gone on for years arguing with you about philosophy or ethics or doctrine, but when you zeroed in on grace, I couldn't resist!"

We'll be talking about that grace throughout this book as we draw on the riches of our inheritance. For now I want to stress four aspects of grace. It is offered before we ask; it is initiative; it is inexhaustible; and it is always sufficient.

PREVENIENT GRACE

Don't miss this splendid word. Prevenient. It means beforehand. When used about grace it means "beforehand" love, acceptance that is given before we feel acceptable, forgiveness offered before we ask, and the Lord's choice of us before we even choose to respond. Jesus said to the disciples, "You did not choose me, but I chose you" (John 15:16). This is grace. In Romans Paul wrote, "But God demonstrates His love toward us, in that while we were still sinners, Christ died for us" (Rom. 5:8). This too is grace.

Paul never lost the sheer wonder of the fact that he was a persecutor of Christians when Christ confronted him on the road to Damascus. A few days later Ananias, one of the very Christians he had gone to arrest, introduced Paul to a personal relationship with Christ. Look at Paul's own testimony:

> And I thank Christ Jesus our Lord who has enabled me, because He counted me faithful, putting me into the ministry, although I was formerly a blasphemer, a persecutor, and an insolent man; but I obtained mercy because I did it ignorantly in unbelief. And the grace of our Lord was exceedingly abundant, with faith and love which are in Christ Jesus. This is a faithful saying and worthy of all acceptance, that Christ Jesus came into the world to save sinners, of whom I am chief.
>
> *(1 Tim. 1:12–15)*

I've never met a dynamic Christian who said he or she found Christ, got His attention, and then began a relationship with Him. Rather, they say, "He found me! And even my longing to know Him, He birthed in my heart!" He uses everything that happens to

22

us and around us to bring us to Him. Then Christ whispers, "You are loved now!"

But is grace only for the beginning of the Christian life? Certainly not. In fact, we could not live a day without a fresh supply of grace. Sadly, however, some of us try. We begin the adventure of the abundant life and then try to live on the impetus of our own intellect and physical strength. It won't work! That's when we need the next aspect of grace.

INITIATIVE GRACE

Just as Christ graciously created the desire to know Him, He constantly seeks to initiate a deeper relationship with us. He has to be the one to do it. Often when life becomes pressured, filled with problems and frustrations, we usually try harder to make things work out. When we get burdened down with our failures or sins, we put off seeking forgiveness. We try to be different or better to atone for what we've done, said, or been. Because it's hard for us to admit our difficulties with people, we shift the blame on to them or simply cut them out of our lives.

It's when we neglect His grace that Christ magnificently fulfills one of Isaiah's messianic prophecies, which, by the way, follows the promise of enjoying life. "My elect shall enjoy the work of their hands. . . . It shall come to pass that before they call, I will answer; and while they are still speaking, I will hear" (Isa. 65:22, 24).

The secret is that Christ motivates in us the desire to pray! He invades our minds with the realization of our need, guides us to the wording of our prayer, and intercedes on our behalf to the Father. When we are at last able to admit our need or confess our sins or seek help with problems, He breaks our bonds and frees us to cry out for help.

INEXHAUSTIBLE GRACE

The grace Christ mediates to us is inexhaustible. We simply cannot diminish the supply. Our prayers are like draining water from the Atlantic Ocean with a teaspoon. And the supply of grace exceeds the waters of all the seas.

We are offered superabundant grace. I like the way John puts

23

it in his Gospel, "And the Word became flesh and dwelt among us, and we beheld His glory, the glory as of the only begotten of the Father, full of grace and truth. . . . And of His fullness we have all received, and grace for grace" (John 1:14, 16).

The word "for," *anti* in Greek, can mean either "in substitution for," or "superseding." I think John is talking about superseding grace. The grace expressed in the Commandments and the Father's persistent, patient mercy revealed in the Old Testament is now superseded in the grace given in Christ Jesus, His atonement, resurrection and Pentecost power.

But let's go further. The word *anti* can also mean "upon." Try that on for real enjoyment! Grace upon grace. This not only describes God's mighty acts in history but in our own personal experience in Christ: grace that He found us; grace that He filled us with His Spirit; grace that intervenes in hundreds of serendipities each day; grace to cry out for Him when we are down; grace to praise Him when we count our blessings; grace when we are ill; grace when we need wisdom and love with people; grace to see us through trials; grace to die victoriously; grace to live forever. Grace heaped upon grace, indeed!

All-Sufficient Grace

As the supply of grace is inexhaustible, it is also all-sufficient. In a time of physical need, Christ's assurance to Paul was, "My grace is sufficient for you" (2 Cor. 12:9). The word "sufficient" here not only means adequate, but also fitting. The grace Christ provides is fit for our needs, perfectly matched for what we are going through in the ups and downs of life. Looking back on what we've faced, we say, "The Lord knew exactly what I needed." This gives us a confident hope for the future. All-sufficient grace, grace that is suited to our specific needs, brings peace.

Peace Happens

Grace is what Christ is. And peace is what happens when we accept that we are loved now. The battle within us is over. Estrangement from the Lord is past. Peace is forgiveness. Peace is trusting. Peace is giving our worries over to Christ and leaving the results to Him. Peace is "equipoise," the equal balance of our needs with the inflow of Christ's love, wisdom, and strength. Again, we hear the whisper, "You are loved now. Peace be in you."

I WILL ALWAYS LOVE YOU

Last year, I took part with another pastor in the marriage service of some friends. The pastor used the old rendition of the marriage vow, ending with the words, "Till death do us part."

The bride smiled, said the words to the groom and then whispered, "I will always love you."

Wonderful words from a bride, a friend.

Always is a long time. Its span includes changes, moods, diminished strength, failures, and hurts. It also includes future problems. When we say this to others we are also expressing a longing for the same assurance from them.

But only Christ can follow through consistently. And His love always begins right now. It's the grace that produces peace.

You are loved now!

4

HOW
TO
OVERCOME
INSECURITY

After I finished my study leave a few summers ago, I relaxed by fishing for a few days near Braemar, Scotland. One afternoon I went into the village and was delighted to see and to hear a bagpipe band of young adults performing in the city square.

Perhaps it was because I felt lonesome for my children that I identified so closely with the pipers and dancers. The chief piper reminded me of my eldest son, Scott, who plays the bagpipes. And one of the dancers with the bagpipe band, either by my imagination or by an exact likeness, looked like my younger son Andrew. A young woman standing in the square in a kilt made me think lovingly of my daughter Heather.

Well, after they finished I couldn't resist telling them how magnificently they played and danced. The father of two of the pipers, who acted as their overseer and director of the band, was a little concerned that I might be too effusive and egregious in my comments. He looked like one of those sergeants who won the Battle of the Bulge.

His firmly set jaw was determined when he said, "Sir, you've got to be careful. You're going to turn those children's heads with all those compliments."

The father's words rumbled around inside me while I was fishing the next day. I had a wonderful "gillie," a guide, who led me to a place where he said I was sure to catch a salmon.

I fished all day. Over lunch we sat down and talked. I had not caught a fish. I told the gillie about my dad and of the great memories I had of him teaching me how to fish. Perhaps the six most wonderful words I heard as a boy were: "That's a grand fish, Lloyd."

That afternoon I resumed fishing. The gillie went off to take care of other matters and was not with me in my moment of triumph when I landed a huge salmon. Admittedly, the fish has gotten heavier and bigger as the years have gone by. Yet as I pulled it up onto the shore—after feeling that at any moment I was going to lose it—I longed for someone with whom I could share the sheer delight of having caught it. I almost felt that maybe dad was there, sharing it with me.

Now, gillies are very formal people who usually address the person they're guiding with the term "Sir" or "Madam," or if they have a title, with "Doctor," or "Professor."

Throughout the morning I had been "Doctor Ogilvie." The gillie had been very kind, though respectfully distant. But when he returned and saw the marvelous salmon, he broke the barrier of propriety. He looked me squarely in the eye and said, "That's a grand fish, Lloyd."

In a sense, the gillie blessed me on my dad's behalf. We all need to be blessed in a deeper way. In this chapter we're going to think about this true blessing.

SECURITY IS BEING BLESSED

Inside each of us is a blessing-shaped void. We are so constituted that we cannot know security until we are blessed. We cannot live with the immense insecurity of the changes of life until we know we are blessed.

In God's strategy for His creation and the building of mature personalities, He has entrusted the gift of blessing to the family. In Israel the father was primary in the giving of the blessing. If you are a parent you know that you cannot give away what you have not received. Your ability to bless is dependent on how much you have been blessed by your own parents. The sad truth is that many of us grow up without the inner child of our past feeling blessed.

The giving of the blessing is the giving of approbation, affirmation, value and belief in a child's future. Without it we cannot live. To a certain degree we may or may not have received this blessing. In the biblical sense the blessing is the giving of the father's birthright to the son or the daughter. Because he believes in them, the father blesses his children with courage and daring to be who they are.

Unfortunately, as we mature, there may still remain a deep insecurity inside us because we weren't blessed. The word "security" comes from the Latin *se-*, meaning without, and *cura*, which is care. To be secure is to be able to live without care, without worry, and without fear. When we have been given security by our family throughout our growing years, we are able to face the insecurities of life. We are equipped to make tough decisions and are able to live with the consequences. This is maturity.

THE GREATEST BLESSING

Yet no person can fill the blessing-shaped void which every one of us feels. No human being, no mother, father, friend, or fellow adventurer in the faith, can give us enough of the blessing to make us secure. Only God our Father can give us this blessing.

A Father-need exists in every one of us. God is our Father, sublimely our Father. He is the sovereign Lord and procreator. He is the one from whom life has come. And as our Father He desires to bless us.

THE BLESSING OF THE FATHER

When Paul wanted the Ephesians to know of their inheritance so that they could draw on it with freedom and delight, he began with helping them to realize that they were blessed. The words came flaming and burning out of the apostle's mind: "Blessed be the God and Father of our Lord Jesus Christ, who has blessed us with every spiritual blessing in the heavenly places in Christ" (Eph. 1:3).

Paul could not contain himself. Initially, because he did not know that he was blessed, he had been a swaggering, arrogant Pharisee. Then he met Christ. The blessing-shaped void in him was filled. This is why he could write to the Romans and declare, "But I know that when I come to you, I shall come in the fullness of the blessing of the gospel of Christ" (Rom. 15:29). Nothing was left out of this blessing. Because Paul was secure in the blessing of the Father, he dared to do things that would cause any human being terrible insecurity.

None of us can live without this blessing. Our lives will be turbulent, filled with a constant succession of anxieties and worries bred in the spirit of fear and trepidation. We will grow introverted and seek to hide behind an exterior bravado that hides the frightened person we are inside.

Paul wanted the Ephesians to know that the Father had come through Jesus Christ to bless and to adopt men and women as His own sons and daughters. He did this so that they might know of His saving love, His redemption, His encouragement, and the fact that He would never let them go.

"Blessed be the God and Father of our Lord Jesus Christ, who has blessed us with every spiritual blessing in the heavenly places in Christ," Paul says. God has adopted us and given us an assurance of our value and of His love. With every spiritual blessing God the Father, reigning in the church in Christ, pours out His power.

What does the Spirit of Christ do in us? He gives us the understanding and the experience of what is the mind of the Father toward each of us. Paul says that what is happening in the heavenly places is now appropriated and given to each of us through the power of the impact of the Spirit in each of our lives.

THE GREATEST MIRACLE

What we are talking about here is the greatest miracle that can happen. When we are convinced that Christ is our Lord and Savior and that we have been forgiven of our sins and are without blame, then He fills us with the power of His Spirit. He takes our brain and molds it around the central fact that *We Are Blessed*. He blesses us with every spiritual blessing in the heavenly places in Christ.

THE MAJESTY OF THE BLESSING

Do you know what this means?

It means that at this moment the Father's love for you and for me is exactly the quality of His love that He has for Christ.

Does this startle you? It does me. Before Christ came the angels sang, "Glory to God in the highest and on earth peace, good will toward men!" The words really mean, "Peace among men with whom God is pleased." And at Christ's baptism God said: "This is my beloved Son in whom I am well pleased."

Throughout His life Jesus Christ reached out to the broken, the lost, and the downtrodden. He also reached out to some up-and-outers. Through their secure exteriors He perceived that the inner child of their past was battered, frustrated, and without blessing. And He blessed rich and poor. He went to the Cross to set them free.

Have you ever heard the Father say to you, "You are my beloved daughter, my beloved son?"

Then He calls you by name and says, "You are mine. I have adopted you."

When He loves us with the power with which He loved His Son, we begin to know the majesty of what it means to be blessed "with every spiritual blessing in the heavenly places. . . ."

Now, the heavenly places are not a geographical location, but a spiritual realm. Though The Lord's Prayer opens with, "Our Father in heaven," the word for heaven in the original Greek is actually plural: "Our Father in the heavens." Our Father is both running the universe and here with us in Christ. He is inside of us in the Spirit that we might know that we are loved.

Once, when I was praying through the meaning of this for myself, I closed my eyes and pictured the face of my dad. He smiled, but with his customary reticence was not able to say what I needed to hear him say in that moment: "Lloyd, you're all right. I love you. I bless you."

I almost wanted to cry out in the midst of the vision of my father's face: "Say it, Dad. Say it!" Sometime later in another time of reflection he did, and I felt blessed.

More important, I have seen the face of my heavenly Father in the face of Jesus Christ. Beholding Him I have heard the

Lord and Creator of the Universe say to me, "Lloyd, you are my beloved."

Tipping the Scales

So, you see, what the Father does is change the balance of the scale of life. On one side of the scale are all the memories of hurt or rejection or failure or the pressures or difficulties of life. They weigh down our self-image until the scale tips to one side. Then the Father comes to us and begins loading the scale with every spiritual blessing in the heavenly places. Suddenly, we see the scale not only balance but tip over completely on the side of the Father. And we know we are loved.

So, if the lame would suddenly walk and the blind see, it would be no greater miracle than when each of us has the deep, inner security of being blessed.

"Just as He chose us in Him before the foundation of the world, that we should be holy and without blame before Him in love" (Eph. 1:4).

Cutting the Taproot

Can you see what the apostle is doing? He's cutting the taproot of our desire to justify ourselves before our Father. Paul is saying that, even before we were born, God loved us as much as He loves us right now. What this understanding does is take away those false feelings that the Father will love us more if we perform correctly. This is not so. It is because of His love for us that we want to do what is His will for us.

Even before the foundation of the world, God chose us in Christ. In His mind, coexisting with Christ, His creative Word, God thought of us. It was because of us that Christ came. This is how much we mean to Him. He came so that we would know that we are blessed, that we would be secure in the depth of our inner being and able to face the adversities, difficulties and problems of life.

Blessed for a Purpose

We move on in Paul's doxology of praise for God's blessing in Christ. God has blessed and chosen us for a purpose. He "predestined us to adoption as sons by Jesus Christ to Himself, according to the good pleasure of His will, to the praise of the glory of His grace, by which He has made us accepted in the Beloved" (Eph. 1:5–6).

Paul heaps up magnificent words to describe the wonder of our blessing. Let's savor the meaning of God's predestination, our adoption, and the good pleasure of His will.

PREDESTINATION

We are blessed because the Father has chosen to choose us. He has predestined us. The word "predestination" has had a lot of bad press through the centuries. We need to clean up some of these serious misunderstandings.

Predestination is not fatalism. The word does not mean that our lives are controlled by some impersonal force. And it does not mean that God has chosen some people to be saved and others to be damned. Also, let me clarify that predestination is not the exclusive belief of Presbyterians.

So what is it? Predestination is the conviction that God is sovereign and that salvation is His gift. The doctrine of election is not only that we belong to God by His choice of us but also that He has chosen to be our God.

The Greek word for predestine is *proorizo*, a combination of *pro*, "beforehand," and *horizo*. Our word for horizon comes from *horizo*. It means the limit, boundary, or focus of our vision.

Now, here's the really good news. You and I are the focus of the horizon of God. And for what purpose? Paul says He "predestined us to adoption." The word adoption is *huiothesia* in Greek. It is a combination of *huios*, son, and *thesis*, a placing. The meaning is that the status and relationship to a father is given to someone who is not a natural child.

ADOPTED

In Ephesus, if a man wanted to adopt a son and have that son take his own name, he had to go before a magistrate three times to ensure that the son really wanted to be his. Paul envisions the Father's adoption as the process by which He came in Christ to lovingly appeal to us to accept His love so that we might be sons and daughters in His family.

33

But Why Has He Done It?

Why has He predestined and adopted us? Paul says it was the "good pleasure of His will." God is pleased to have us in His family. We can bring pleasure to God. And so we are back to our central theme. We have been created, blessed, chosen, predestined, and adopted for God to enjoy and for us to enjoy Him. Even when we drift from Him, He searches for us. And with good reason He wants us to claim and use our inheritance.

A Missing Heir

I remember receiving a phone call from a lawyer. He said, "I'm looking for a particular young man. We haven't been able to find him, but I want to tell him he's a very rich man. He is the sole heir of his father's estate. Can you help me find him?"

I knew that the young man was living somewhere in Philadelphia. I traced him through some friends and finally located him in a rundown hovel of an apartment. He was living in squalor.

When I talked to him he said, "Oh, yes, I know Dad's dead. As a matter of fact, you know, we had a broken relationship and I slipped into the back of the sanctuary when you had the memorial service. I didn't sit with the family because, uh, I'm kind of the black sheep."

He paused a moment, then spoke again. "Dad died before we ever got things worked out."

"My friend," I said, "your dad loved you and he left everything to you."

The young man was living a wretched existence when he was the heir of hundreds of thousands of dollars.

Only the Blessed Can Bless

I had a caddy in Scotland whom I asked, "John, where do you live?"

"I don't live here," he answered.

"Oh? I understood that you'd been here a while," I replied.

"I've lived here for forty-five years," he said, "but I no belong."

"Why not, John? How old are you?" I asked.

"Sixty-five," he said, "but I no belong."

My curiosity now thoroughly aroused, I asked, "What would it take for you to belong?"

"I would have been born here and lived here every moment of my life, but I no belong."

I thought of the religious people I know who are in the church and are trying to live good, responsible lives, but because they have never accepted the Father's blessing through Christ, would have to honestly say: "I don't belong." But they can. The blessing is offered.

Someone once said, "The elect are the whosoever will and the nonelect are the whosoever won't."

I think this clarifies the matter. We can take the inheritance given to us or we can refuse to accept it. But do you know what happens when you accept it? You can become a blesser. Only the blessed can bless.

BREAKING THE CYCLE

You see, what happens through Christ is that the cycle of the generations is broken. He has intervened to bless us and fill that blessing-shaped void inside of us. He makes us secure so that in our relationships with family, friends, associates in the church, and people at work we can become those who express blessing, value, esteem, and hope.

A church in the East published its policy by stating, "We reserve the right to accept everybody."

I like this expression, for the acceptance of God in Jesus Christ really means the continuous "gracing" of us, the pouring out of this grace upon us in unlimited measure so that we can be gracious and affirming and uplifting of other people.

Do you know you're blessed? Would you like to know this? Being blessed is the greatest of all miracles. The Father simply places His hand on you and says, "You are mine."

own blood. To the Hebrew, blood and life were synonymous. A person's blood was his life. Christ gave His life for us on the cross as a ransom for our sins.

We are further plunged into wonder about our redemption when we ask, "To whom was the ransom paid?" To answer that we need some background.

We were created for fellowship with God, not as puppets on a string, but as persons with the free will to choose to love, glorify, and obey Him. God's most daring choice was to give us freedom to choose to accept His sovereign Lordship over our lives. To guide us in how to obey Him and to glorify Him, He gave us the Ten Commandments. He asked for complete obedience in having no other gods before Him and in honoring Him in all our relationships.

We know what humankind did with this freedom. Beginning with Adam, the sad tale of history is a long saga of rebellion, resistance, and recalcitrance. Yet, God persisted amazingly in His blessings and love. He called Israel to be His chosen people and gave them His blessing. Throughout the Old Testament we see God wooing His people with love, yearning over them, intervening for their deliverance, and providing for their needs. In each period of this history we hear the loving heart of the Father calling out to His children. We hear His voice in the prophets who announced both judgment and mercy and predicted a time when God would send His Messiah. And those who listened to these prophets heard what Emmanuel would come to do. He would be the Lamb of God for a cosmic atonement for sin.

In His holiness and love God could not wink at sin. He could not compromise either His justice or His mercy. Therefore, out of grace He sent His Son "to demonstrate . . . His righteousness, that He might be just and the justifier" (Rom. 3:26). God set the ransom price by His judgment of sin. By God's mercy, He came in Christ to pay the full price, and at the cross, exposed His heart. God abhors, condemns, and judges sin, and yet by the power of the cross, He forgives sinners—people like you and me!

I am even more awestruck when I understand the meaning of the words Paul uses to identify our human condition and our abject need for forgiveness.

5

OH, THE WONDER OF IT ALL

Some of my fondest memories of my mother involve discussions of our faith during the last year of her physical life. Our visits woul always end up talking about grace and the cross.

Her final comment would be, "Oh, the wonder of it all, the wonder of it all!"

Mother was overwhelmed by Calvary!

One evening at a conference I thought of her exclamatio wonderment at the love and forgiveness of the cross. It was a stirring moment. I was deeply moved by the impact of the pr ing of the cross by a friend of mine and the singing that foll Everyone in the auditorium, I'm sure, felt with me the won outpouring of love, peace, hope, and power.

As I walked out of the auditorium, I listened with int the various reactions of people to this liberating message heard about Jesus Christ. Most of the comments were approving. However, one woman's words startled me. T in stark contrast to the way I felt and thought ever would feel.

The word Paul uses is *paraptoma,* which means to transgress, or "to fall aside." This implies getting off the path or going over the demarcation line into what has been forbidden. We have all gone over the line in breaking the Ten Commandments and Jesus' commandment to love. We've brought hurt, pain and suffering to ourselves and others by what we've done or said or refused to be. We've broken His heart. And even before we asked Him, He forgave us. He reconciled us. He exonerated us. We stutter out our yearning to be free in response to His cross, melted by His love, and healed by His forgiveness.

The same voice that cried, "Father forgive them," from Calvary, says to us with the commanding power of His cross-shaped heart, "The ransom has been paid for all time. And now in this propitious moment in your time it is a pardon for you. You are forgiven. You are free!"

Oh, the wonder of it all, indeed!

Without the liberating experience of our redemption, there's no real beginning of the Christian life. Without an hourly, daily return to the wonder of Calvary, there's no lasting transformation.

Perhaps the reason so many Christians are underwhelmed is that they stop at the beginning. The cap is slapped back on the telescope of their vision and the lid jammed back down on the potential of what Christ could do with them if they trusted Him completely.

We are too quickly satisfied with too little of what Christ offers to us, so we turn back.

We climb over the barbed-wire fence Christ has set up around our old self and return to the concentration camp of willful self-control. We wish what Paul described as the riches of His grace, "which He made to abound toward us in all wisdom and under-standing" (v. 8) was true for us.

The word "abound" is one of Paul's cornucopian expressions for abundance. Christ's redemption penetrates our thinking about ourselves, others, circumstances, life, and death. We are given an abundance of wisdom and prudence. The word Paul uses for wis-dom is *sophia.* Wisdom is the gift of the indwelling Spirit, beyond intellect and understanding, that enables us to know the plan and purpose of God and to discern His will.

41

Prudence, on the other hand, is *phronesis,* the application of wisdom to human affairs. It is the sound sense that helps us to see not only what needs to be done, but how to go about it.

We need both *sophia* and *phronesis* every hour of our lives as we grow in our redemption. God gives us an abundance of both. As we recognize the needs within us and surrounding us, God will give us the wisdom and the prudence to hear what He is saying about them.

People around us will say, "That's magnificent! I never thought of that possibility and the way you carried it off." We will know the answer was a supernatural gift.

But let's move back to Paul's main trend of thought in these Ephesian verses. He's moving along on a very specific track at high speed. His thoughts are rushing toward a grand conclusion. We are given redemption to leave the concentration camp of sin, self-centeredness, and pride. Instead, we are given the gifts of wisdom and understanding for a reason. We are loved and forgiven, enabled and equipped to be a part of a new people participating in seeing and cooperating with God's plan for our lives and all of history!

THE MYSTERY OF HIS WILL

God has "made known to us the mystery of His will, according to His good pleasure which He purposed in Himself, that in the dispensation of the fullness of the times He might gather together in one all things in Christ, both which are in heaven and which are on earth—in Him" (vv. 9–10).

A "mystery," as Paul uses the word here, is something which is known only to the initiated, the inner circle. As redeemed saints, we are shown the Father's plan for us and the rest of human history.

A single word unlocks the mystery: oneness. God's strategy is to unify us with our potential self from whom we have been estranged by our self-hate. Furthermore, God wants to reconcile us with others in profound love and forgiveness. Ultimately, He wants to unify in harmony all races and nations in which men and women, nature, heaven, and earth live in a new Eden.

This is what Jesus prayed for on the eve of His crucifixion. "I do not pray for these alone, but also for those who will believe in

Me through their words; that they all may be one, as You, Father, are in Me, and I in you; that they also may be one in Us, that the world may believe that You sent Me. And the glory which You gave Me I have given them, that they may be one just as We are one. I in them, and You in Me; that they may be made perfect in one, and that the world may know that You have sent Me, and have loved them as You have loved Me" (John 17:20–23).

With confident trust in the Father, Christ prayed and then went to Calvary as the answer to His prayer. His cross was for the atonement of men and women with God and each other, for Jews and Greeks, slaves and free, rich and poor.

This is what Paul means in Eph. 1:9 "by the mystery of His will." God is at work through the present, living, reigning Christ to accomplish His purpose. Note that Paul says that it is His good pleasure to do so because He enjoys accomplishing God's purpose. And He's called us to enjoy being part of His grand design.

POWER FOR OUR PURPOSE

If we ever needed a clear description of our vocation as saints, Paul provides it in verse 12: "That we who first trusted in Christ should be to the praise of His glory." "Being" precedes "doing." We who have been ransomed and released are given power to *be* praise. We are not just to give praise but *be* praise.

This means that we live out the faith in a way that expresses our praise, and also instigates praise in others. We are to be a living demonstration of what Christ can do with the raw material of a human being.

Perhaps this even means that when others see what Christ has accomplished in us and does through us for unity, they might say, "Oh, the wonder of it all!"

But this will require taking the cap off and blasting the lid off our reservations.

The next step in this process is to receive the gift of the sealing that uncaps. So press on!

6
THE
SEALING
THAT
BLOWS
THE
LID
OFF

As you read the title of this chapter, you probably said to yourself, "Either that's a misprint or Lloyd is just trying to be clever with words."

Neither is the case. Rather, I want to tell you about a sealing that blows the constricting lid off of our lives.

In the previous chapters I've alluded to the metaphor of the lid on our expectations and our potential. In this chapter I want to explain and illustrate more fully what I mean. In Ephesians, Paul describes this as the "sealing of the Holy Spirit." When we are sealed by the Holy Spirit, we enjoy God with the lid off our reservations.

"In Him you also trusted, after you heard the word of truth, the gospel of your salvation; in whom also having believed, you were *sealed* with the Holy Spirit of promise, who is the guarantee of our inheritance until the redemption of the purchased possession, to the praise of His glory" (Eph. 1:13–14, italics added).

What is this sealing with the Holy Spirit? Note that Paul clearly states it is subsequent to hearing the gospel and believing. It is a gift offered to all who have trusted Jesus Christ as Savior and Lord. The lives of many Christians, however, indicate that they may have heard and believed the gospel but have stopped there. They have yet to experience the sealing of the Holy Spirit. Some background on this metaphor of sealing is helpful.

In Paul's day, people used a seal on an object to indicate ownership. Sealing was done by dripping hot wax onto an item and then pressing a person's seal into it. The seal was the name, crest, identifying brand or initials of the owner. People sealed valued documents, letters, and objects. This practice was common in sending official papers, crates, and packages, because the seal clearly identified the sender. If someone took a trip, the possessions he took with him would be sealed to protect them from theft or loss. If the belongings were sent ahead of him, they could be identified and claimed when he arrived at his destination.

We get a clue to the spiritual meaning of sealing from Jesus' words about His own sealing. In John 6:27 he said, "Do not hunger for the food which perishes, but for the food which endures to everlasting life, which the Son of Man will give you because God *has set His seal on Him.*" I believe Jesus was referring to His baptism. "Jesus, when He had been baptized, came up immediately from the water; and behold, the heavens were opened to Him, and He saw the Spirit of God descending like a dove and alighting upon Him. And suddenly a voice came from heaven saying, 'This is My beloved Son, in whom I am well pleased'" (Matt. 3:16–17). This was the special anointing of the divine-human Son of Man. Though He knew He was the Son of God, this was the authenticating sealing by the Father.

How magnificent! The divine Son of God, living in human flesh, exemplified the sealing that He would be designated by the Father to give to all those who accepted Him as Savior and Lord after His resurrection and glorification.

And, so, the sealed Son of God promised, "If anyone thirsts, let him come to Me and drink. He who believes in Me, as the Scripture has said, out of His heart will flow rivers of living water" (John 7:37–38). The disciple John who recorded the words clarified, "But this He spoke concerning the Spirit, whom those believing in Him would receive; for the Holy Spirit was not yet given, because Jesus was not yet glorified" (v. 39).

46

John the Baptist prophesied how this would happen. "I indeed baptize you with water; but one mightier than I is coming, whose sandal strap I am not worthy to loose. He will baptize you with the Holy Spirit and with fire" (Luke 3:16).

After the Ascension and Christ's glorification, He did indeed return and executed the Father's entrusted authority as Lord of the church to be the baptizer of believers with the Holy Spirit and fire. The persons of the Godhead worked in perfect oneness: the Father as sovereign of all creation, the Son reigning as Lord and Savior, and the Holy Spirit dwelling in the believer. The Father adopts, the Son redeems us and the Holy Spirit seals us.

Now we are ready to bring together the image of sealing objects and the sealing of the Spirit. He gives us the gift of faith to believe in Christ. "No man can say that Jesus Christ is Lord except by the Holy Spirit" (1 Cor. 12:3). Then the Spirit seals us. He melts the wax of our souls and presses into it the seal of Christ. The result of this sealing is confirmation, conformation, and conflagration. Here's how it works.

The sealing of the Holy Spirit confirms for us that we belong to Christ. His seal of ownership is on us forever. It declares to whom we belong and that our ultimate destination is heaven. We become sure of our salvation and are set free of furtive doubts about our faith. But that's only the beginning result of the sealing.

Next we are conformed into the image of Christ. With His seal pressed into our being—thinking, character, values, and goals—we become more and more like the One who owns us.

Then the seal brings zeal. A conflagration, a great fire, begins to burn in our hearts and minds through the sealing of the Spirit. The fire is fueled by undeniable convictions, an unextinguishable warmth for people, an unbridled passion to live for Christ, and an unconquerable expectation for the future. People who have been sealed by the Holy Spirit are ready for anything, without reservations. It's the infilling of the Spirit, a baptism of power, an anointing of vision and hope.

The sealing of the Holy Spirit blows the lid off!

Now, the crucial questions: Do you know many lid-off Christians? Would you count yourself among them? Why are there so few Christians today living with the assurance, the Christlikeness and the fire of the sealing? In short, what keeps the lid clamped tightly shut?

OUR OWN CLAMPS ON THE LID

Unfortunately, many contemporary Christians have clamped the lid on their own freedom and expectation. It could be said that they trusted in Christ after hearing the gospel of salvation. But sadly we could not say that they have been sealed with the Holy Spirit of promise. The assurance and power of the Spirit is lacking. They try to live their faith by human effort. This is the plight of half-sealed Christians with only half of the gospel.

Now this is not the fault of Christ. He does not choose some people to be filled with the Spirit and other people to live out their salvation on human strength. No, something else is the cause.

Some people are the victims of incomplete biblical instruction. They were never told that the baptism of the Spirit—the anointing with power—is either necessary or possible. Preachers and teachers can lead people only as far as they have gone themselves. And frankly, many of them do not include the blessing of the Spirit-filled life in their proclamation of the gospel.

But something else is the cause for others. Even when the Spirit-filled life has been included in their introduction in Christianity, people still miss the power of the Spirit. I think it's because of our petulant proclivity as humans to try to control our lives even after we've become Christians. And so, the Christian life becomes a strenuous struggle of self-effort.

After the initial enthusiasm of becoming a Christian, we return to running our lives. We might be certain that Christ died for our sins and that we will go to heaven at death, but living between now and then becomes an arduous task. The obligatory "oughts" and "shoulds" for being good people are increased with the added challenges of Christian ethics and responsibility. We can become religious without the Spirit. And with the grimness of living on our own strength we never discover how to enjoy God.

Now, with all theological terminology and theories brushed aside, I need to ask: Are you living in the flow of supernatural power from the Spirit? Are you being anointed with the Spirit daily, for each task, each challenge? Does He abide in you?

Both my own personal pilgrimage and years of working with people who lack power prompt me to ask these questions with tenderness and urgency.

STOPPING AFTER THE FIRST STEP

Of the three steps to dynamic Christian living—salvation, security, and strength—I find Christian clergy and laity all over the world who have stopped at the first step.

Many Christians need the sealing of the Spirit to be absolutely sure they belong to Christ and to receive His strength to become courageous disciples. I think a sure sign that we need this sealing is evident when we have limited God by clamping down the lid on what He can do in us and in our churches. The truly dynamic Christians I know had a time of being broken open and then being filled by the Spirit.

Many Christians attest that this happened when the challenges of living the Christian life on their own strength became impossible, or some problem was too great to solve, or some opportunity too immense to tackle. Sometimes they had to make an honest admission of inadequacy at a time of failure. Some had cried out for strength in some debilitating illness. And still others, upon reading the biographies of great people like Wesley, Whitefield, Moody, and others, discovered that these men had a time after conversion when they were particularly anointed with the Spirit. Then they spoke with boldness and lived with courage. We say, "Lord, I want this power!"

FROM BLANDNESS TO BOLDNESS

Recently, during a pastoral staff meeting at my church, we discussed how this transition from blandness to boldness happened in our lives. Every one of these leaders had experienced a time after becoming Christians when they realized their spiritual impotence. When they cried out for Christ to help them, He intervened and made them sure of Him and His supernatural strength. They experienced the anointing of the Spirit and claimed His transforming power in them and in their ministries.

An elder at my church realized his need for the sealing of the Spirit long after he committed his life to Christ years ago. His exemplary character and generosity made him a shoo-in for nomination and election to eldership. However, no one knew how uncertain he was about his relationship to Christ because he had kept that hidden beneath a polished exterior. He didn't anticipate that being part of the elders' prayer ministry at the end of our worship services would confront him with his own insecure relationship with Christ. When people came to pray with him, he keenly saw that something was missing in his own life. He had never allowed Christ to break through his inner hard shell of self-sufficiency. Being called to minister to others forced him to see that he was in over his head spiritually. What he was asked to pray for in others he needed himself.

Fortunately, my friend began to talk about his spiritual emptiness, although it was not easy for him to admit his neediness. He had spent his entire life convincing others that he was adequate.

As we talked, I shared with him the power of the Spirit-filled life. He'd heard hundreds of sermons about the Spirit, but the words never penetrated his shell. Now Christ was breaking the shell, allowing my elder friend to receive what Christ had longed to give him for years—the Spirit. We knelt and prayed together while he asked to receive the security and strength of being sealed. And Christ was faithful. Into the soft wax of this man's ready heart, He pressed the seal of His indwelling presence. A religious leader claimed his inheritance.

PRONEWAL

The sealing of the Spirit provides pronewal. Pronewal? Yes, pronewal!

It's for those who do not have a previous experience of the Spirit's power to revive or any former intimacy with His presence and ability to renew. Pronewal is exactly what this coined, compound word suggests: "Pro = forward; newal = newness." When our inner nature is yielded to the seal of Christ pressed into our souls, we experience pronewal. And when that happens, we are given a forward thrusting sense of newness.

BLOWING THE LID OFF

Now, we are back to where we started. The sealing of the Spirit blows the lid off our restrictions on what can happen in our lives. The imprint of His sealing opens us to dare to imagine what He can do with our lives. What's more, we are filled with the Spirit to venture out to attempt what may have seemed impossible before.

THE DEPOSIT OF HEAVEN

Paul speaks of the sealing as a guarantee of our inheritance. The word he used means "an earnest deposit, a down payment in like kind." The apostle says that the sealing is a down payment "until the redemptions of the purchased possessions." Life in the power of the Spirit is a foretaste of heaven.

I like to interpret the down payment of our inheritance, the sealing of the Spirit, as only a beginning. Receiving the indwelling power of the Spirit is followed by our being transformed by the fruit of the Spirit. Christ's character is formed in us—love, joy, peace, patience, kindness, goodness, faithfulness, gentleness, and self-control. We are showered with the gifts of the Spirit for courageous ministry: wisdom, knowledge, discernment, healing, praying for and expecting miracles, and more.

The sealing of the Spirit took place in my life five years after I was converted. I couldn't live the Christian life on my own strength and asked the Spirit to live in me. He gave me a tremendous excitement for living. I wrote out a motto and by the Spirit's power have tried to live it ever since: "Each day lived as if it were my only day will equal a life lived at full potential."

So, more important than yesterday or what tomorrow might bring is living with the lid off today!

spiritual eyes do not comprehend or appreciate. Having eyes, we cannot see.

Conversion begins the healing of our heart-eyes by removing our spiritual cataracts. We understand what the cross means for our forgiveness, but we still do not perceive all that the Lord has planned for us and the power He has offered to us.

We need a supernatural lens implant in the eyes of our hearts. Our vision continues to be impaired.

How graciously Paul exposed this need in the lives of his readers! He did not reprove them for their lack of vision, but shared what he was praying for them to receive. He confronted them only after he had affirmed their faith, their love for one another, and his gratitude for them. The apostle knew that affirmation must precede reproof.

The heart-eyes of the Christians of Asia Minor needed enlightenment. Their inner eyes needed to be dilated to receive the greater light of truth about Christ. But for them—and us—this truth requires the refracting power of the lens implant that I'm talking about.

Paul calls this lens the "spirit of wisdom and revelation." In some of the ancient Greek manuscripts the "s" of spirit is capitalized, which is consistent with the unveiling of truth in the work of the Spirit within us. The Spirit is the lens for the eyes of our hearts. He makes us wise. Wisdom is the mind of God as thought through us by the Spirit. We have been created to know God and to think His thoughts after Him. With the lens implant of wisdom we can see things as God sees them, express the emotion of praise, and will to become cooperative in the fulfilling of His will.

What are we to see with the Holy Spirit implant of wisdom? Paul enumerates three magnificent things.

THE HOPE OF OUR CALLING

First, we are enabled to grasp the "hope of His calling." Paul has established that our calling is to be saints. He wants us to see the hope that sainthood gives us.

Hope is more than wishing, yearning, or optimism. As it is used in the Bible, the word "hope" means confident expectations rooted in the Lord's promises. Hope never exists by itself. It springs forth in response to His gracious assurance, "For I know the thoughts that I think toward you, says the Lord, thoughts of peace and not of evil, to give you a future and a hope" (Jer. 29:11).

In Ephesians Paul uses the word "hope" in relation to the plans of God for us focused in Christ. These plans are that we know Christ, be filled with His Spirit, and consistently become more like Him. We are given a clear picture of the person we are meant to be. In spite of our vacillating human nature, Christ pushes us forward. He loves us as we are, but never leaves us stagnant. He empowers us with hope, based on His promise that He will never leave us or forsake us.

More than this, we are given confident hope that He will use all that we go through to enable us to grow in maturity as saints. Nothing is wasted. With this hope we can endure the pressures and pain of adversity.

Hope is not something Christ *gives;* it is what He *is.* We receive lasting hope when He lives in us. This quality of hope makes us resilient, confident, and bold. Because Christ never gives up on us we can endure without giving up.

Let's listen in on the apostle Paul's prayers:

> Therefore I also, after I heard of your faith in the Lord Jesus and your love for all the saints, do not cease to give thanks for you, making mention of you in my prayers; that the God of our Lord Jesus Christ, the Father of glory, may give to you the spirit of wisdom and revelation in the knowledge of Him, the eyes of your understanding being enlightened; that you may know what is the hope of His calling, what are the riches of the glory of His inheritance in the saints, and what is the exceeding greatness of His power toward us who believe, according to the working of His mighty power.
>
> (*Eph. 1:15–20*)

We note that this New King James Version of Paul's prayer uses "eyes of your understanding." In the Greek text we read, literally, "eyes of your hearts." Heart, in biblical usage, is the whole inner being—intellect, emotion, and will.

The hope of our calling not only assures us strength for each day, but a fearless attitude toward death based on Christ's promise that as He lives, we shall live also, now and forever. We can look at death as little more than a transition in the midst of eternal living. With the lens of wisdom implanted over the cornea of our thinking, we can face the future unafraid, with hope.

A part of our calling is not only to see with hope, but to become communicators of hope. Living our hope makes us attractive, contagious people in a hopeless world full of people who are thrashing about with uncertainty. Our privilege is to be ready to share with everyone our "reason for the hope that is in us" (1 Pet. 3:15).

CALLED TO BE SERVANTS

These opportunities will come to us as we live out another aspect of our calling: to be servants. Being a servant is one of the least claimed blessings of Christians. We have been called to give ourselves away to people. This means involvement with them. It's patiently listening while they sort through their feelings and thoughts; it's caring for them even when it is inconvenient; it's giving our time, energy and money when needed; and it's being willing to be vulnerable in revealing how Christ has helped us in our own problems.

It is also something more. The witness of a communicator of hope must be authenticated by an active ministry of meeting the needs of people in a suffering society. We earn the right to be heard when we live out our faith—not only by compassionate caring for individuals, but in working for social justice, feeding the hungry and battling the problems of poverty and addiction which hold people captive.

The lens for the eyes of our heart not only enables us to see what Christ did for us and the person we are destined to be, but also lets us focus our eyes on other people. We now can see the depth of their need and the height of their potential. We can see problems for what they are and envision what Christ can do with them. And hope overcomes our complacency about the church, our community and our nation, and gets us moving on the Lord's agenda.

Proverbs reminds us that as we think so we are. "For as he thinks in his heart, so is he" (Prov. 23:7). We become what we think about. All of us are in the process of becoming what we envision we are destined to become.

The hope of our calling is to contemplate the immensity of the Lord's plans for us. Our problem is that we think far too small. To think with the lens of the Spirit of Christ refracts by His power our vision of what's possible. He gives us a microscope to examine the present and a telescope to envision His future for us and others.

His Inheritance

To see clearly, we must know "the riches of the glory of His inheritance in the saints." Here's a glorious thought to contemplate and to live with delight—You and I are Christ's inheritance. If the pronoun "His" refers to Christ, the new lens-implanted eyes of our heart behold what we mean to Christ.

We have been thinking about what Christ means to us. Let's allow our minds to soar for a moment about what we mean to Him.

Jesus often spoke about those who believed in Him as the Father's gift to Him:

> All that the Father gives Me will come to Me, and the one who comes to Me I will by no means cast out. . . . This is the will of the Father who sent Me, that of all He has given Me, I should lose nothing, but should raise it up at the last day. And this is the will of Him who sent Me, that everyone who sees the Son and believes in Him may have everlasting life.
>
> (*John 6:37–40*)

With wisdom-implanted eyes we see the interaction of the Father and the Son. Just as those who believed in Jesus during the Incarnation did so by the Father's work in their hearts, so too Christians believe by the inheritance of the reigning Christ. By divine election the Father sets us apart and makes us part of the "legacy of the liberated" entrusted to Christ. Though we don't realize this prior to our conversion this is why we are attracted to the gospel, drawn magnetically to the cross, and propelled irrevocably to the risen, reigning Christ to claim the promise of our ransomed freedom. With releasing joy we leave our bondage and fall reverently, adoringly at the feet of King Jesus. Now we are His to enjoy.

At this point our role changes. We are not only cherished subjects of the King's domain, but we are the conscripted troops of a conquering Commander's invasion of realms that belong to Him but resist His rule. We are called to be crack spiritual commandos for the invasion of the bastions of evil. And with Christ in command, the gates of hell cannot prevail against us (Matt. 16:18).

Being part of Christ's inheritance is the essence of *our* inheritance. To belong to Him, to be called to serve in His battle for righteousness, and to know that we cannot ultimately be defeated is a substantial inheritance. You were elected to be given to the Son so that you could give your life to Him, so that He could be His gift to others and eventually lift you to heaven and present you to the Father. Can you picture this at every stage? If not, ask for a lens to be implanted into the eyes of your heart.

Just words? They may appear to be until we see the power available to make them a reality.

EXCEEDING GREATNESS OF POWER

The third thing we are enabled to see is the abundant power available to us. Power is elusive. We feel its influence but find it difficult to grasp. But with the lens of the Spirit we can see authentic power. God has shown us in an actual display of strength the nature of the power available to us. Note the way Paul describes what we are able to see: "What is the exceeding greatness of His power toward us who believe, according to the working of His mighty power which He worked in Christ when He raised Him from the dead and seated Him at His right hand in heavenly places, far above all principality and power and might and dominions, and every name that is named, not only in this age but also in that which is to come" (Eph. 1:19–21).

With the new eyes of our hearts, we can see the power offered to us. Yes, we are able to look at the empty tomb. God's power raised Jesus from the dead, out of a dark tomb into the glorious light of eternity. Then it placed Him at His right hand of power. This position is not just geographical. It is the designation of authority to reign as Lord of all. As Jesus came and embodied Himself in humanity, He came back to live in us. He fills us with His own Spirit and enables us to be His agents to extend His work in our relationships and responsibilities.

And there is more. For the living out of our life in this portion of eternity, we are given the same power that raised Jesus from the dead. This is awe-inspiring!

How does this power really work? First, the Lord heals the faculty of memory in our brain. With the implant of the lens in our heart, we are able to look back on our life refracted into precise focus through the cross. We then see everything we have done or said that is self-incriminating, that holds us back, that makes us feel negative about ourselves, and that fills us with hurting memories. The Lord sees it too and, with the power of His love and forgiveness, cleanses all of it away.

Can you look back on the whole of your past and know that you have been redeemed and set free, that you have been forgiven and never need return to self-hate? If not, the Lord now seeks to implant a lens in the vision of your brain which will enable you to look back and forgive yourself.

And what about life in the present? I talked to a man once who said, "I can't imagine that I spent my life without the anointing of the Spirit of God on my brain! I have been making decisions on the basis of my own natural talents, insights, and understanding, but without the vision of what the Lord wants and what He can do. Now that I have received the Spirit's power in my mind, I think about and look at things differently."

This man has received the gift of discernment. Now he can really see the facts. But he always sees these facts in the light of what Christ has done, is doing, and will do. Christ is ready to help him think with power.

Do you have this power? Do you have the discernment of Christ when you look at people? Or, do you shove them into a limiting category? Would you like to see what they can be? Only the Spirit of Christ can give you this. He wants to. It is a miraculous spiritual gift.

How about situations? Do you view them in the light of what could happen if the situation would be infused with the power of the Lord? I don't know about you, but I need this every hour of every day to see what the Lord is ready and willing to do.

The Lord has even more in store for us. In our brain is the capacity of imagination. He gives us the ability to picture things in His love and in the light of His will.

I remember a woman telling me, "My deepest need and struggle is to know the will of God." I realized that although this woman is a Christian who has been sealed in the Spirit, she has never yielded her brain to the Lord.

"Lucy," I asked her, "what is the most important part of you?"

She answered, "Well, I guess since thinking controls everything, it would be my mind."

"Think of your mind as a kingdom," I suggested. "Who is on the throne of that kingdom?"

"Well, I guess I am," she said. "I never thought of that."

In the midst of having coffee, we stopped and prayed that Christ would anoint her thinking. "Lord, I surrender the kingdom of my mind," Lucy began.

Marvelous things have happened to Lucy. Magnificent new understanding and discernment have been given to her in the raising of her children, in the way she relates to her husband, and in planning for the future. She has become a wonderfully free person. The same power that raised Jesus from the dead is at work in her brain.

Paul continues. As God raised Jesus from the dead, He placed Him above all principality and power and gave to Him a name that is above every name in this age and in every age to come. As reigning Lord He fills all in all.

The Father commands all. *Christ* is present to reign in the church. *His Spirit* dwells in us to help us think His thoughts and to give us freedom from the past, discernment for the present, and vision for the future.

How would you like a lens implant in your heart? Wouldn't it be magnificent to see as God sees? The greatest need in every life is to know God. Do you know Him? Do you know of His wonder? His majesty? His glory? Have His attributes been reproduced in you? Goodness? Love? Grace? Mercy? Forgiveness?

Wisdom? Vision? We have only begun. All it can get is better. The old hymn says:

> Open my eyes that I may see,
> Glimpses of truth you have for me.
> Place in my hand the wonderful key,
> That will unlock and set me free.
>
> Silently now I wait for you,
> Ready, my God, your will to do.
> Open my eyes, illumine me,
> Spirit divine.

The spiritual lens implant in our heart is finished. Take off the bandages and see. It's wonderful to have new eyes!

8

EASTER
EVERY
HOUR

One Easter, after leading worship, I headed for my car. On the way, I saw two young men who had been addicted to hard drugs. Through a decisive encounter with the resurrected, reigning Christ, they had been freed from drugs and had remained free from them for more than a year.

They hailed me as I was about to get into my car. "Hey man, thanks for the Easter fix!" one of them said.

"The what?" I asked, noting that the young man was off drugs, but not the street jargon.

The other man contradicted his friend, "You're wrong. We didn't get a fix, we got hooked up for intravenous feeding from the Man. We're mainlining it on the Lord Himself!"

We all laughed. I appreciated their effort to express what the Easter celebration had meant to them. I reflected on our conversation a lot that afternoon.

There's a difference between an Easter fix and a constant flow of Easter power to really get us fixed up.

Easter is like a fix to many of us. We receive little inspirational injections that block life's pain for awhile. But the fix doesn't last.

We are really agnostic about the power of the resurrected Christ. We don't know the implications of His crucifixion and resurrection for us as the secret of triumphant Christian living.

We may claim forgiveness through the cross and feel some vague relief from our panic about death because Christ was raised from the dead, but what's missing is our own crucifixion and resurrection. Now!

Tom, a fellow adventurer in resurrection living, moved from simply believing in Christ's resurrection to experiencing the transforming power of his own spiritual death and resurrection. He told me, "Lloyd, what a difference! Now Easter is every hour for me!"

Tom is claiming one of the most liberating aspects of his inheritance. He's an Easter person who enjoys God. But to get where he is, he had to go through the narrow door of death to self before he arrived at the wide-open reaches of resurrection living.

The full potential of this transformation is described by Paul in Eph. 2:1–9. He helps us use our new eyes that we talked about previously. He paints a vivid portrait to see our life before and after a personal crucifixion and resurrection. This reminds us of what life is like when we are dead to God, and what life can be like when we are fully alive to God.

THE DEAD AMONG THE DEAD

Prior to our own spiritual crucifixion and resurrection, we are the spiritually dead among the dead. Paul shows us what it's like being a part of the living dead.

> And you He made alive, who were dead in trespasses and sins, in which you once walked according to the course of this world, according to the prince of power of the air, the spirit who now works in the sons of disobedience, among whom also we all once conducted ourselves in the lusts of our flesh, fulfilling the desires of the flesh and the mind, and were by nature children of wrath, just as the others.
>
> (*Eph. 2:1–3*)

The problem of being spiritually dead is that we don't recognize it in ourselves or in others. Think of how often we exclaim, "that's really living!" about lifeless popularity, prosperity, and human power.

There's a humorous story about two gravediggers who were responsible for digging the largest grave they had ever dug. The grave was fifteen feet long and six feet wide.

Throughout the digging, they complained about the size of the grave and wondered what kind of casket was going in it. When they finished, they stood beside the grave and leaned on their shovels. Soon, a hearse drove up carrying the casket, the funeral director, and the attendants. No family or friends of the deceased attended!

The gravediggers wondered why they had dug such a large grave for such a small casket. Their bewilderment grew when a great crane rolled up and stopped beside the grave. When a trailer truck for transporting cars arrived with a magnificent, gigantic, gold-plated Rolls Royce resting on its bed, their surprise turned to astonishment.

The gravediggers watched as the funeral director got out of the hearse and, with the help of the funeral attendants, placed the casket next to the Rolls Royce. They then opened the door of the car and the lid of the casket. Next, they lifted the fully embalmed, neatly dressed corpse out of the casket and placed him on the fine white leather driver's seat. They took his dead, stiffened fingers and wrapped them around the steering wheel. They molded his frowning face into a smiling face. Finally, the director opened the corpse's eyes which looked out on the world with a cold, blank stare.

At this point, the crane swung into position and hooked its metal cable to the top of the car. It then lifted the gold Rolls Royce with the dead man behind the wheel into the air, carried it to the grave, and lowered it in.

One of the gravediggers glanced at the other, looked at the Rolls Royce and said, "Man, that's living!"

THE LIVING DEAD WE ADMIRE

Once I was standing outside a movie theater during the premiere night of a new film. A successful actress got out of her limousine and swept past the crowd in all of her glittering magnificence. The person standing next to me said, "Wow! She's really living!"

The next week the actress was dead from an overdose of barbiturates.

Often, we look admiringly at the beautiful houses of other people, observe the accoutrements of their accomplishments, and say, "Wow, that's really living!"

We see someone in a position we want and we exclaim, "Oh, if I had that power and recognition, I could really live!"

We admire entertainers, great financiers, and government officials, and think to ourselves, *That's what life is all about.*

Our admiration of the facsimile of life among the spiritually dead exposes our misplaced values. Taking a personal inventory sometimes enables us to examine the strength of our spiritual life. We might ask ourselves these questions:

- Is our life a deathless life that a physical demise cannot end?

- Or, are we living in the process of dying, hour by hour, which leads nowhere but to a physical death that locks us into a limbo existence for the rest of eternity?

- How sure are we that we will spend eternity with Christ?

- In other words, are we living in heaven now, so that if we were to die today, death would be a simple transition to the next step of our eternal life?

LIVING DEATH

Paul wanted the Christians in Asia Minor to understand that God had resurrected them from among the living dead and made them truly alive. He longed for them to be sure that they were the living among the dead rather than the dead among the living. In just a few verses, he reviewed what life is like without Christ, without the assurance of eternal life, without resurrection power, in short, without hope.

Essentially, a living death is life apart from God. No one is born into a right, natural relationship with God—we are part of a fallen creation. We are born with a sinful nature, separated from God. Furthermore, Paul says, we were "dead in trespasses and sins."

We encountered these two words earlier in our discussion of Eph. 1:7. Remember that sin, *hamartia,* means to miss the mark by falling short of a clearly defined standard. We sin when we are separated from God, are willfully independent and are negative about the blessings of life. A trespass, *paraptoma,* is a wrong step, a determined crossing of a boundary into a forbidden territory marked "no entry," a deviation from a path we know we are to follow.

In his description of the spiritually dead, Paul points to three dominating incarcerations that keep them "alienated from the life of God" (Eph. 4:18).

Paul used three words to explain the cause of this spiritual death: the world, the devil, and the flesh.

THE COURSE OF THE WORLD

First of all, to be spiritually dead is to walk "according to the course of the world." By "course," we mean, "age," the current period of time in our world. "World" means "society," the organized life of humankind apart from God. "Walk," as Paul uses it here, is a Hebrew word for lifestyle, behavior, or way of living. He is talking about a life lived according to the values, purposes, and goals of culture. The spiritually dead are committed to their culture rather than to God. They are cramming life into the short span of existence on earth with no thought of where or how they will spend eternity.

A CONNIVING PRINCE

Second, when we are dead spiritually, we are under the control of the "prince of power of the air"—Satan. Unfortunately, this includes a lot of nice as well as nasty people. Satan's simple strategy is to separate people from God. He does this by locking us into the syndrome of satisfaction with life as it is and with goals in keeping with culture. Satisfaction with secondary securities becomes a substitute for knowing God—our primary security.

More perversely, Satan is the source of the evil that is congealed by the patterns of a humanistic society. Good people who are spiritually dead frequently become unknowing channels of Satan's schemes. They not only wink at evil, but actually become active participants in perpetuating customs that uplift materialism and downgrade righteousness. Whenever people are dehumanized, moral absolutes are discarded and people are denigrated, then Satan wins. He collects his trophies when people become obsessed with things, sex, power, and manipulation. And he's no less satisfied with combative competition, prejudice, hatred, gossip, and envy.

Satan's ultimate design is to make people think that what they have is really living and to spurn the idea that God's way is a better way to live. If Satan can convince a person that this life on earth is all there is, he accomplishes his goal. When he does, people become imprisoned.

FLESH IS MORE THAN SKIN DEEP

Third, a further manifestation of a living death is the longing, lusting quest for the desires of the flesh. The meaning of "flesh" in the Bible is more than skin-deep. In fact, its roots are in the depth of our being. "Flesh," as Paul uses the word here, is another way of saying self-centered living under our own domination. Eventually, we don't feel a need for God and we certainly don't want Him meddling in our affairs. Finally, we become defiantly determined to run our own lives.

THE GRACE OF WRATH

Paul says that people under the sway of the course of this world, the influence of Satan, and the addiction of the flesh are "by nature children of wrath." This means that the spiritually dead are following the natural inclinations of human nature as part of a fallen humanity. By nature, we are self-centered and do not desire God.

The exercise of our willful independence causes a particular expression of God's grace—God's wrath. You may be surprised that I associate grace with wrath. I do it because wrath is the righteous, holy indignation and judgment of God against our pride and the arrogant sinful things we do because of it. If God did not love us, He would not care. But because of His gracious love, He judges us and shocks us with the truth of what we are doing with the gift of life that He has given us. Sometimes He allows the consequences of our attitudes and behavior to take their natural course in order to enable us to realize our plight.

God condemns self-righteousness in all its blatant and subtle forms. We become uncomfortable with life without Him. He allows us to see the truth about ourselves so that eventually we can see how much He loves us and experience His mercy.

Would it be grace to let us go? Would it be love not to confront us and to leave us among the living dead? No! He confronts us and propels us toward experiencing Easter every hour.

But God!

Now we are ready for Paul's exclamation, "But God!" Despite our dead spiritual condition, He has mercifully intervened to raise Christ from the dead and, through Christ, to raise us out of our tombs of sin, fear, and anxiety. "But God, who is rich in mercy, because of His great love with which He loved us, even when we were dead in trespasses, made us alive together with Christ (by grace you have been saved), and raised us up together, and made us sit together in the heavenly places in Christ Jesus, that in the ages to come He might show the exceeding riches of His grace in His kindness toward us in Christ Jesus" (Eph. 2:4–7).

If we had no more than these three verses, we'd have the essence of our inheritance. God has saved us, resurrected us, and adopted us. The propitious parenthesis, "by grace you have been saved," is the source of everything else.

In the Greek, "saved" is a perfect participle which signifies the continuing results. We have been saved, we are being saved, and we will be saved forever. The word "saved" means deliverance, wholeness, and healing. All this takes place when we accept Jesus Christ as our Savior, receive forgiveness, and are set free of guilt and condemnation. This is when we are miraculously raised up out of a living death into a deathless life. We are alive forever.

But our salvation is not the only dynamic. We are raised up to a new level of life: life in Christ and Christ in us. Our resurrection is not simply a refinement of old talents and abilities, but a new creation, not just a different attitude, but a new spirit, the Spirit of Jesus Himself. In Gal. 2:20, Paul says, "It is no longer I who live, but Christ lives in me; and the life which I now live in the flesh I live by faith in the Son of God, who loved me and gave Himself for me." This is when "Easter every hour" begins and never ends.

I think this cycle of continuing commitment and resurrection is awesome. Every hour of our life we face opportunities, problems, perplexities, challenges, and people with immense and often seemingly impossible situations. When we surrender them to the Lord, in our discouragement and often our defeat, He raises us up and gives us supernatural power to know what to do and to say.

In every crucial relationship I've had, I've been brought to the place of surrendering my own plans and desires to manipulate and control. The Lord consistently restores my relationships with His grace in the center.

A few months ago, I had a breakdown of communication with a close friend. We both were to blame. The tension mounted. Finally, I committed the whole problem to the Lord. In silent listening for His response, I was shown what I had to do. I had to humble myself and ask for my friend's forgiveness. When I did, he told me the Lord had given him marching orders to seek *my* forgiveness! Out of the ashes, a new relationship was born!

But the Lord's intervening, resurrection power is given not only for life's impossible problems, but also for our immense opportunities. There's always a time when we get to the end of our strength and courage and have to surrender the future of a plan, project, or program.

We cry out, "Lord, help me! I can't do it alone!" Easter happens again.

Out of the grave of our depleted efforts, the Lord gives fresh vision, insight, and answers we had not conceived of before. For resurrection living there is resurrection power and hope to live each hour!

PERSPECTIVE AND AUTHORITY

We can live with courage because we have been raised up and given the privilege of sitting together with Christ "in heavenly places" (Eph. 2:6). This is the secret source of an hourly Easter. The term "heavenly places" means the unseen world of spiritual reality. From the perspective of heaven we look on our earthly struggles. In prayer, we are lifted out of our present pressures. We are shown what God is doing to us and to others, and what He is ultimately planning for us. We become heavenly minded so we can be of greater earthly good!

And where do we sit? On a throne! Christ's throne. This is what He promised the Laodiceans in Rev. 3:21, "To him who overcomes I will grant to sit with Me on My throne." In the light of Paul's reference to sitting in heavenly places, we can claim this promise now. While we are on earth, we also are sitting on the throne. From it we can see what Christ wants done and accept the daring authority He entrusts to us to move into action.

A BEAUTIFUL PERSON

After reiterating his basic theme that we are saved by grace through faith, Paul concludes this section of his epistle with another grand assurance: "For we are His workmanship, created in Christ Jesus for good works, which God prepared beforehand that we should walk in them" (Eph. 2:10).

The word for "workmanship" is *poiema,* which denotes "something that is made," and often refers to a thing of beauty and perfection. Our English word "poem" comes from this word. A poem has flow, symmetry, order, and balance. We have been created for nothing less. The Lord wants to shape the beautiful person He intends us to be. Seeing our potential, He wants to move us to a heavenly perspective from where we can look with amazement at our new self and on the good works He has planned for us to do.

This is Easter every hour, not a temporary fix, but an intravenous feeding of love and hope from Christ's heart to ours. *This is living! This is enjoying God!*

9

WHEN THE WALLS COME TUMBLING DOWN

John has discovered the way to establish immediate rapport. When he first meets someone he asks, "Are you feeling better?" One day I heard him ask a waitress that question.

"Yes, I'm feeling much better," she replied. "As a matter of fact, my headache is gone and I'm over the flu."

Surprised by the response, I asked John, "Do you know her?"

"No, not at all," he explained. "I just know that most people feel badly. If you ask them if they are doing better, they usually say 'yes' or 'no.' The next thing you know, you're into a conversation."

John has also devised a wonderful way of developing friendships at a conference with people he does not know. He first squints at a person's nametag to learn his first name. Let us say the man's name is Tim. Later, when he sees Tim, he says, "Hello, Tim. Is that situation solved?"

Tim responds, "How did you know about that situation?"

Immediately they are in a great conversation and a friendship begins.

Each one of us is getting over something or has faced some difficult situation, challenge, or opportunity.

WE ALL NEED PEACE

A deep need exists in all of us for an abiding, unchanging, profound peace. I am concerned that so many people who are Christians do not have this peace.

At this moment, do you have a deep, inner sense of calm? Do you have a feeling of well-being? Do you sense the everlasting arms of the Lord around you, reassuring you that whatever you are facing or going through, you will be all right?

There is a wonderful story about a piccolo player who was the most faithful in attending the rehearsals of an orchestra. For months, he devotedly followed the guidance of the conductor.

One day the conductor, wanting to make an example out of this fine man who was so conscientious in his attendance, said to his orchestra, "I want you to be like this piccolo player. Always here. Always faithful."

The piccolo player raised his hand and replied, "Sir, I want you to know that I can't make the performance, but I've been here at all of the rehearsals just to make up for it."

I know many "piccolo player Christians" who are at all the rehearsals, but won't be at the performance. They have not discovered the reality of God's peace in their lives. There are still walls in their hearts.

EXPERTS IN WALLS

One summer day, while I was driving along an old country road in the Highlands of Scotland, I passed a stone quarry with a shed beside it. Outside the shed was a sign that read, "A. J. McIntyre, Stonemason. Expert in building and replenishing walls."

Driving on, I thought to myself, *I know a lot more people than A. J. McIntyre who know how to build and replenish walls.*

Our walls cause our lack of peace. We construct them to protect ourselves even in early childhood when we discover how to have secrets from our parents. We also learn how to separate our inner life from our outer life. We hide things about ourselves from others. Brick by brick our protective walls grow higher. Soon these walls become a castle surrounded by a wide moat. It is not long before the moat bridge of the castle is up. We raise a victory flag, though inside the castle we are alone, lonely, and uncertain. As long as walls exist between us, God, our real self, and other people, we have no peace.

In this chapter, I want us to look at these walls and what it means to have them come tumbling down. Jesus Christ, the Prince of Peace, came to destroy these walls. In Eph. 2:11–22, Paul mentions peace three times. He tells us that Christ is peace, that He has made peace, and that He makes us peacemakers. Christ's peace is part of our inheritance to enjoy.

As a basis for teaching us how to experience peace and be a peacemaker, the apostle Paul uses a historic situation. He talks about the historic conflict between the Jews and the Gentiles and about the walls that had separated them. "But now in Christ Jesus you who once were far off have been made near by the blood of Christ. For He Himself is our peace, who has made both one, and has broken down the middle wall of division between us" (Eph. 2:13–14).

When Paul speaks of the "middle wall of division," he is referring to the wall between the court of the Gentiles and the courts of Israel in the ancient temple. Inside the temple was the Court of the Women, the Court of Men and the Holy Place, where the sacrifices were performed. Beyond this was the Holy of Holies, an area separated from the Holy Place by a thickly woven, heavy veil. Behind the veil in the Holy of Holies was the Ark of the Covenant, which contained the tablet of stone on which the Ten Commandments were carved. Once a year, on the great Day of Atonement, the high priest would sacrifice a lamb on the altar in the Holy Place just outside the Holy of Holies. Then he would go behind the curtain and offer the blood of the lamb to God for the sins of the people. No one else had access to this most sacred place.

Gentiles were not permitted beyond the court of the Gentiles. On the thick wall separating it from the rest of the temple was a sign clearly stating in both Latin and Greek, "Anyone passing this point will be prosecuted and put to death." This very sign was found by archaeologists when they excavated the wall of partition in 1817.

When Jesus Christ died upon the cross, His completed work of atonement and reconciliation through the shedding of His blood ripped open the curtain separating the people from the

Holy of Holies. Spiritually, the middle wall of division between the Gentiles and the Jews was also destroyed. Christ did this by the power of His own love and forgiveness.

CHRIST IS OUR PEACE

It is in this context of Christ's death that Paul writes. First, Christ is our peace. The prophets of the Old Testament predicted His coming as the Prince of Peace. In Isa. 57:19, which I think is the Old Testament basis of this section of Ephesians, Isaiah quotes the Lord as saying, "Peace, peace to him who is far off and to him who is near, says the Lord, and I will heal him," which means, "Peace, peace, to the Gentiles and the Jews through My Messiah."

In Isaiah 9 Jesus Christ is described as the Prince of Peace. His ministry was to bring profound peace, but at a high cost— the cross.

Wherever Jesus went, He obliterated the historic walls that separated people from one another. Note the walls that He destroyed in His personal ministry prior to the cross. First, He called not rabbis or priests, but twelve laymen to be His disciples. Then He taught them that their ministry was not only to the Jews, but also to the Gentiles. Instead of skirting Samaria, Jesus always traveled through it, ministering to those who were called half-breeds and hated by Israel.

Jesus ministered to women, caring for them as persons. His forgiving love was offered to tax collectors and prostitutes. Then He went to the cross. As He shed His blood, Christ destroyed the walls that separated the people from the Father, from each other, and from their own deep inner self.

Thus, Paul says, "For He Himself is our peace, who has made both one" (Eph. 2:14). Christ is peace. He not only gives peace, He *is* peace. There is no way that we can know peace apart from Him. Christ's peace is the peace of forgiveness. It is the peace of pardon. It is the peace of acceptance.

All through this passage, Paul talks about the cross as the agent of bringing peace. Our inner heart can have no peace until we know that we are absolutely and unreservedly forgiven. If we are jangled or feeling unsettled, it is because something in us has not been forgiven and healed. The good news of the gospel is that Jesus Christ forgives us before we ask to be forgiven. Let me underline a point I made earlier: *We confess our sins because we know we have been forgiven, not that we may be forgiven.*

Deep inner peace comes from cleansed memories, clear purposes, and the knowledge that nothing stands between us and the Lord. Have you built a wall against Him? It is amazing how many Christians have. We worship, give, attend church activities, call ourselves Christians, and work for Christian causes, yet inside we often are a cauldron of unsettled feelings, unresolved guilt, fears and frustration.

We all need to receive into our lives the Peacemaker, the Prince of Peace. He will take hold of our hearts, lead us down the stairway of our memories into that castle dungeon where we keep all the hurts of the past. He says, "Give your hurts to *Me*. Let *Me* take them away with the power of the blood of *My* forgiveness."

Experiencing lasting peace through Christ is more than forgiveness of the past, however. Christ also confronts our self-justification and self-righteousness. The enmity between the Jews and the Greeks stemmed from the arrogance of the Jews. They were proud of being God's people. This fostered exclusivity and superiority. Their confidence was in how well they had kept the Commandments and the thousand and one little rules and regulations the Pharisees and scribes had written for living. Keeping every minute detail led to self-righteousness and spiritual pride on their part. The wall dividing the Jews from the Gentiles not only was in the temple—it was built in their hearts.

This also is the plight of religious people. We have a brief and fleeting experience of God's love and forgiveness, then spend the rest of our lives assembling rules, regulations and standards that we can point to and say, "Here, God, finally I have earned your love." But instead of giving us peace, He exposes our pride, for peace cannot be earned.

INDWELLING PEACE

The peace of Christ comes when He dwells in us. "Peace I leave with you, My peace I give to you," Jesus says, "not as the world gives do I give to you" (John 14:27). Christ wants to be certain we understand that His peace is not just the sensation we feel when everything happens to be going our way or, when for a brief time, there are no major problems on our horizon or when we reach some plateau in our mad scramble to climb the ladder to a success we might envision or even when we acquire some level of economic security. Christ's peace is more profound than a resolution of external conflicts.

When Christ says, "Shalom," He means it as more than a greeting. Peace is His life, His death, and His message combined. It touches a human life with forgiveness, acceptance, and freedom. When Christ comes to live in us, He resolves our fears, quiets the storms within us, and sets us at peace. Only then can we go about being peacemakers.

Until we have Christ's peace, we cannot reconcile relationships with others. We cannot bring harmony to a marriage, to a church, to a community, to a nation, or to the world. We are far off the mark if we think that a new bill in Congress, an innovative governmental decision, or a laudable cause will suddenly bring peace. This is not the way peace happens.

As we see in this passage, peace comes first through the person of the Savior, second through the pardon of His cross and, third, through His entrance into us to resolve our inner conflicts. The same progression follows our ministry. Filled with Him we become peace in our relationships. When He resolves our own inner tension, we are able to go to people with love and acceptance. We are able to model and then mediate the grace of Christ's unqualified forgiveness.

The question remains: "Are we willing to forgive the way Christ forgives?" He forgives before people ask to be forgiven. Have you forgiven everyone who has ever hurt you, even though they did not ask? How about in your marriage? How about with your children or with your parents? Or how about that person who has spitefully misused or manipulated you or tried to scuttle your hopes and dreams?

To be a peacemaker means to go to a person with love and acceptance to communicate forgiveness, regardless of whether he or she deserves it or even receives it. Only the peace-giving of Christ makes possible the union of people who would otherwise be separated and fragmented from each other.

DIVISIONS IN THE CHURCH

We live in a time in Christendom when the Church, the body of Christ is polarized into the fundamentalists, the evangelicals, the charismatics, the social activists, and the institutional champions. Each group shouts from inside its own castle, "I've got the answer!" And each misses the point that we need each other.

The Peacemaker is seeking to do a magnificent thing in our time. He is calling together a new breed of biblically rooted, converted people who are filled with the Holy Spirit, who care about society and who are faithful to their churches. This is a new day. The Peacemaker is creating it. He is calling us to dismantle the walls that divide us.

How often we hide in our own little fortresses, however. If we are fundamentalists, we scrutinize what other people believe about the Bible. If we are evangelicals, we ask, "Have you been born again?" Those of us involved in society ask, "Have you put your life on the line for a social issue?" If we happen to be in the charismatic community, we query, "Do you speak in tongues?"

If anyone answers us incorrectly, then that person cannot enter our castle. We draw up the moat bridge and secure the ramparts for battle. It becomes a battle nobody wins. And those who really lose are the people in our society who need to see that Christianity can work to bring peace in and between people.

THE PEACEMAKER ON THE MOVE

One of the most exciting things happening in the greater Los Angeles area is a new movement the Peacemaker has instigated to bring Christian leaders out of their secure theological and denominational castles.

Two years ago, a small group of pastors began meeting for breakfast. We are an interracial group of pastors from high and low churches, rich and poor churches, traditional, evangelical, and charismatic churches. The two things we have in common are our commitment to Christ and our deep concern for our city, its people, and its problems. We came together with no other agenda than to pray for Los Angeles.

When we first met together, sharing our needs and praying for one another, the walls came tumbling down. We grew in a profound love for each other.

Then a vision was birthed among us. Why not become the inviting committee to call all the pastors and church leaders in Los Angeles together for a prolonged time of prayer? A list was assembled and the invitations were sent. The date set was February 14, Valentine's Day. The proposed four-hour prayer time was called, "Shepherds Love L.A." Because of the central location of the Hollywood Presbyterian Church, we had the privilege of hosting this unprecedented gathering.

WHAT THE PEACEMAKER DID

I remember the excitement and anticipation I felt when I drove to the church at 6:00 that morning. Would anyone come? What would be the attitude of people from so many different backgrounds?

My heart leapt with joy as I saw cars streaming into the parking lot. When I reached the fellowship hall where my elders and deacons were serving breakfast for the pastors, it was already full. *But how would the prayer time go? Could all these leaders find common ground in Christ, forget their differences and be galvanized into a mighty prayer army for Los Angeles?* I wondered to myself as I talked to many over breakfast.

At 7:00 A.M., we moved into the sanctuary and began the four-hour prayer time. I was stunned by the size of the crowd. More than 1,300 people had gathered to pray!

We spent the first hour in guided prayer for our own needs as people. Small groups of four were formed for mutual intercession for each other. The walls between us crumbled as we opened ourselves and shared honestly our hurts and hopes for our lives as individuals and as leaders.

The next hour was spent praying for our churches. The mutual trust, established by the personal sharing, freed us to confide our concerns and boldest dreams for our churches.

Then, in the following hour we turned the focus of our prayers to the gigantic needs of our city. Microphones had been placed in the aisles on the main floor and the balcony in the sanctuary so we could hear the prayers of one another. People lined up at the microphones and, one by one, led the great assembly in prayer for the gripping needs of our city—the problems of the street gangs, runaway teens, prostitution, pornography, poverty, hunger, the homeless, and the new wave of prejudice. These are only a few of the many needs brought to the Lord in prayer.

Several times the prayers called us to repent for our lack of involved caring and commitment to Christ's agenda of reconciliation and healing. Often, we had been part of the problem and too seldom part of the Lord's solution. Tears were shed as we cried out for Christ to revive His church with new passion for evangelism and mission.

The final hour we spent praying for the vision and power to get us moving as a united church. Again the prayers flowed with intensity interspersed with spontaneous singing when someone would begin a hymn or prayer chorus and the whole group would join in.

The meeting ended at 11:00 A.M. with the singing of "All Hail the Power of Jesus' Name." The suggestion that we meet again was unanimously approved. At the time of this writing, two more meetings have been held with the same great number attending and the same uniform purpose: to pray for our city.

Miraculous things have happened not only in answered prayer but in the oneness Christ has forged between us. We are an interracial, intercultural, interdenominational fellowship without walls. And who knows where it will lead? Only the Lord knows, and His plans exceed our wildest dreams!

I have shared the story of this contemporary experience of what the Peacemaker is doing because it vividly illustrates what Paul wrote about peace in this passage from Ephesians. As pastors we claimed and received a part of our inheritance we had neglected. We now know that our peace in Christ is inseparably related to being in peace with one another and being committed to claim God's promise in Jer. 29:7: "Seek the peace of the city where I have caused you to be carried away captive, and pray to the Lord for it; for in its peace you will have peace."

The Peacemaker wants to bring us into oneness and wholeness. He yearns that we experience all that He has to give.

Do you know His peace? Or are you like the piccolo player who had been at all of the rehearsals, but missed the performance? If you know the peace that passes all understanding, are you a conduit of that peace in the world? Does your marriage suffer a discord that you could heal if you were the first one to say, "I'm sorry"? Are you involved in a power struggle where you work? Are you trying to manipulate people to do your thing to your music and to your timing? What would it mean to let the Peacemaker live in you and to be a peacemaker yourself?

In Phil. 4:6–7, Paul wrote, "Be anxious for nothing, but in everything by prayer and supplication, with thanksgiving, let your requests be made known to God; and the peace of God, which surpasses all understanding, will guard your hearts and minds through Christ Jesus."

There's a lovely story of a little girl who once had to recite this marvelous verse. But toward the end of her recitation, she got it mixed up. Standing before her fifth-grade class, she said, "The peace that passes all misunderstanding."

This is the peace I am talking about.

10

TRIUMPH IN TOUGH TIMES

One day, a group of us had a wonderful time remembering the songs we had sung in Christian youth camps. My friend George Henricksen came up with one I had never heard before.

> Down in the dumps I'll never go,
> For there the devil makes me low.
> So I'll pray with all my might,
> To keep my armor bright,
> So down in the dumps I'll never go.

What do you do when you discover yourself down in the dumps? Some of us pray that our armor might be bright, yet we still experience those times when we feel low.

TOUGH TIMES

Life has its tough times. Though we try to live as faithful, obedient disciples of Jesus Christ, sometimes life's pressures get us down. We feel fearful and frustrated because we are uncertain whether we'll make it or not. Do you ever have such times?

only hope is Christ. Then I could say with Count Zinzendorf, "I have one passion. It is He! It is He!"

That quality of passion for Christ overflows in a profound concern for people.

THRILLING PRIVILEGE

The second reason Paul could triumph in the tough time of his imprisonment in Rome was that he thought of his primary calling in life as a thrilling privilege. He goes on in Ephesians 3 to share his astonishment over the privilege he had been given. The apostle was amazed that in spite of his persecution of the Christians, the Lord had chosen and called him and given him faith to believe that He was Israel's Messiah. That would have been enough for him to spend the rest of his life in praise and thanksgiving. But the thing that constantly stunned Paul was that he had been called to spread the gospel to the Gentiles. Consumed by the wonder of that, he humbly saw himself as a steward and servant of the grace of God. He could take whatever happened to him because he saw it as a further opportunity to express his privilege of being a communicator of grace to people.

Feel the pulsebeat of that liberating sense of privilege: "You have heard of the *dispensation* of the grace of God which was given to me for you. . . . I became a *minister* according to the gift of the grace of God given to me by the effective working of His power. To me who I am less than the least of should preach among the Gentiles the unsearchable riches of Christ" (vv. 2, 7, 8, italics added).

The word "dispensation" means stewardship. The role of a steward was to oversee the management and distribution of his master's resources. Paul was profoundly moved by the privilege of receiving grace and being appointed to share it with others. His stewardship was lived out as a minister. The word means servant. As a steward and servant of his Master, the apostle poured himself out unstintingly. He knew he was a part of the Lord's strategy for the evangelization of the world and that His grace always would be sufficient in the difficulties he faced. In life's tough times, Paul focused on the privilege of grace rather than the problem which could have caused him grief.

The same can be true for us. A sure way to triumph in a

tough time is to think of it as a signal to stop and think about our privilege to experience and communicate the grace of our Lord. Nothing will pull us out of the dumps faster than remembering that we belong to Him, that His love will never change, and that He will use the very tough times we're in to enable us to grow in His grace. Life is a school of grace. If the curriculum were limited only to the easy times, we'd remain in first grade forever.

How we handle our tough times determines how effectively we are able to communicate grace. When we can see the problems as an opportunity to become empathetic, sensitive communicators, our tough times will lose their power to keep us in the dumps. Instead of praying glibly, "Lord, get me out of this tough time," we are able to ask humbly, "What new depth of grace can I get out of this tough time?"

Paul's phrase, "the stewardship of God's grace given to me for you," is a great motto for life's tough times. Everything that happens to us is not only for our own personal growth in grace but for our ministry to others.

My friend Allan is discovering this secret. He's in the computer business, but his real vocation is helping people experience the Lord's grace. Recently he shared a discovery he's made about tough times.

"Lloyd, it's amazing, I've had a succession of opportunities to talk to people who were facing some tight places in their lives. It's startling to realize that the Lord has used the very things I'd learned in similar situations to help me identify with them and share what He can do to help them. So now when things get tough and I have to trust the Lord more than ever, I also get ready for the next person He puts on my agenda. Usually it's somebody who needs what I've just discovered. What a privilege!"

When growing in peace and communicating it to others becomes our purpose, all of life can be looked on as a privilege. The very things and people who could put us down in the dumps become part of our privilege.

For example, think of those times when responsibilities pile up, the pressure grows and we get bogged down. Sometimes when my desk is piled high with work and I can't imagine meeting all the deadlines, I think, *Why am I doing all this?* I've learned over the years that the only way out of a dumpy mood like this is to reflect on the privilege of being alive, of being a recipient and communicator of grace, and of working for God's glory. Then I say to myself—and anyone else who will listen—"It's a privilege!" And it becomes just that. It is a privilege to write a letter of encouragement, to author a book, and share grace with people who need it so desperately.

Few things will transform our attitudes toward people who cause us tough times than to think of the privilege we have of being stewards and servants of grace to them. The triumph over our rotten feelings about them begins as we can say inside ourselves when we are with them, "It is a privilege to know and love you in spite of our problems. I consciously make a commitment to seek to be to you what Christ has been to me."

What about tough circumstances? We're not to think of problems as privileges, are we? No, but to tackle them with courage and wisdom from the Lord is certainly one of our finest privileges. We are prisoners of the Lord, not our problems. The central issue of any problem is discovering what the Lord wants us to do and then to do it as a privilege.

If we exercise our privilege of knowing the Lord and living with His guidance for our actions and decisions, we can count on His faithfulness. He will keep us out of many potential problems. When we stumble into problems because we did not listen, He will help us out of them. But there are other problems He uses for our growth in grace. Then, too, there are problems in the lives of people and society in which He calls us to be His agents.

But whatever the nature of the problem, our only questions are, "What does the Lord want? What does grace demand of me in response? What would I do if I didn't hold myself back? If I were not trying to conserve my pride, protect my image, or save face, what would I do? And if I saw Christ-inspired problem solving as a privilege, what would my attitude be?" These questions are wonderful steps out of the dumps of tough times.

TRANSFORMING POWER

Third, Paul could triumph in the tough time of his imprisonment because of the Lord's transforming power. In verse 7 he speaks of the "effective working of His power" in his own conversion and call to ministry. That same power through Christ transformed the apostle's imprisonment into an opportunity for "effective working" in others. Prayer was Paul's source of the consistent flow of power. He says in verse 12 that in Jesus Christ our Lord "we have boldness and access with confidence through faith in Him." The apostle could pray with boldness and confidence because he believed that through Christ he had direct access to God. The word "access" is *prosagoge* in Greek. The word means to lead a person into the presence of another, and the person is accepted on the basis of the merits of the introducer. Prayer in Jesus' name brings us the same favor and acceptance as is given by the Father to the Son.

No wonder Paul felt boldness, the freedom to say all that was on his heart, and confidence, the assurance that what he prayed could be answered with an outpouring of fresh power. The result was that the apostle had boldness and confidence to live in his tough times. Through these experiences Christ led him to the very heart of God and the source of power in his difficult circumstances. He wrote Philippians, Ephesians, Colossians, and Philemon, as well as 1 Timothy, during his first imprisonment.

Paul did something else. Many of the guards who were chained to him were converted to Christ. Caesar constantly had to replace the apostle's guards because under the apostle's influence they were becoming disciples of Christ and followers of the Way. Caesar's household was becoming Christian. In an attempt to curb Paul's influence Caesar had to remove many of the guards and transfer them to Roman legions throughout the empire.

Imagine being chained to the apostle Paul! The guards had the opportunity to see authentic Christianity at work. They had to listen to Paul's prayers, dictations of his epistles, and conversations with other believers. Knowing Paul's contagious faith, we can picture how he must have focused love and care on each of them. Paul was an irrepressible personal evangelist. Every guard was a potential disciple of Christ.

We are left to think of the people bound to us not with Roman manacles but with the bonds of family, friendship, partnership in work, and association in the activities of our communities. Many of them are watching us closely to see what our faith means, not only in our successes, but in our tough times. Often we contradict what we say about Christ in easy times by the way we fall apart in tough times.

It doesn't have to be that way. We have the same access to power Paul had. And Christ our eternal intercessor constantly goes to the Father on our behalf and brings from the Father supernatural power so that we too can have boldness and confidence.

In this passage of Ephesians we've had the opportunity to visit Paul in prison to learn the three secrets of triumph in tight places: We can have the triumphant perspective of being a prisoner of the Lord and not circumstance, we can experience the thrilling privilege of growing in grace, and we can receive transforming power to turn obstacles into opportunities.

How It Works

Last year during a tough time I was going through, my dear friend, Hester Caldwell, who had been raised in a missionary family in China, shared with me a moving account of how Alice and James Hudson Taylor experienced triumph in a very difficult time in their lives in China during World War II.

The Taylors were missionaries and had placed their four children in a school in Chefoo in the Shantung Province while they continued their work in the interior. Then when the Japanese invaded China, they were separated from their children for a prolonged time without any information on their well-being. Horror stories of the Japanese occupation of the Shantung area reached them, but no word about the children. Meanwhile, Alice and James had to continue their work with the people in their area who were suffering from epidemics, starvation, and homelessness.

Alice and James were engulfed with anguish over their children. "Oh, dear God, my children, my children" Alice cried out as she prayed for their safety.

One day, while kneeling beside her bed praying for the

children, she reached out to God in a prayer of complete surrender of the children to His care. His answer came in a very stirring way.

A LIBERATING MEMORY

Alice was carried back in memory to when she was sixteen in Wilkes-Barre, Pennsylvania. She pictured her pastor, Pa Ferguson, sitting there telling her words he had spoken years before: "Alice, if you take care of the things that are dear to God, He will take care of the things dear to you." This was the pastor's translation of "Seek first the kingdom of God and His righteousness, and all these things will be added to you" (Matt. 6:33).

Alice pondered the words. The Chinese people to whom she and James were called to minister were dear to God. And her children were especially dear to her. They were all dear to God. A deep peace replaced her agony. Alice reaffirmed her commitment of the children to God's care and threw herself into her work with renewed dedication.

In spite of the distressing news that all the children and teachers of the Chefoo School had been captured and crammed into a concentration camp, Alice held on to the promise—if she took care of the things dear to God, He would take care of the things dear to her. "My strength is God's strength," she would assert with confidence. "I know He will not forsake my children."

GOD'S MYSTERIOUS WAYS

Five and a half years later, after the Japanese surrender, the children were released and eventually reunited with Alice and James. They had survived the difficult years in the concentration camp where they had continued their studies under their missionary teachers.

Indeed, as Alice and James took care of the things dear to God in the war-ravaged land—teaching, feeding the starving, and caring for the wounded—God had taken care of their dear children.

I have retold the story of Alice Taylor's prayer triumph in a very tough time to share this remarkable promise available to all of us. It's true, "If you take care of the things dear to God, He will take care of the things dear to you."

Paul knew that. He had confidence that God would care for the Christians in Asia Minor as he cared for the things dear to God in his imprisonment in Rome. And the same has been the bold confidence of the saints through the ages in their tight places.

We were meant to do more than survive. We can triumph in tough times!

11

MORE
THAN
YOU
EVER
IMAGINED

Two years ago I fell in a hiking accident in the Highlands of
Scotland. My left leg was badly crushed. After a long time in bed,
I had to learn to walk all over again. The pain was excruciating
and the emotional trauma was debilitating. Thousands of people
wrote me from around the world to tell me they were praying for
me. I couldn't have made it without their prayers.

One day, a friend by the name of Milt saw me limping and
wincing with pain. He took me by the arm and said, "Lloyd, I'm
really, I mean really, praying for you."

My friend is one of those people who say what they mean and
mean what they say. He is known for his economy of words and
usually understates his feelings. For him to say "really" was sur-
prising, but for him to repeat the adverb was amazing. What he
was trying to communicate was that he was praying with great
earnestness.

In an even more dramatic way the apostle Paul told the Christians in Asia Minor that his prayers for them were more than
fleeting moments of intercession. He wrote, "For this reason I
bow my knees to the Father of our Lord Jesus Christ" (Eph. 3:14).

What is so special about this? A great deal. As a Hebrew, Paul usually prayed from a standing position. But he told the Christians that when he prayed for them he bowed his knees. "Bowing the knees" was a phrase used to express prostrating yourself. He wanted the Christians to know the deep earnestness of his prayers for them. Calvin believed that Paul was in this consecrated position of prayer as he dictated to his scribe.

Imagine it. Paul's wrist was chained to his guard. For Paul just to get on his knees would have required the guard's permission and cooperation. But for Paul to prostrate himself, the guard would have had to get down on the floor with him. Perhaps the guard was one of those Paul had led to Christ. If not, hearing the prayer the apostle prayed would have been instrumental in his conversion.

What Paul prayed, recorded in Eph. 3:14–21, is one of the most eloquent and inspiring prayers in the Bible and in all literature. Inspired by the Spirit of God, true prayer begins with God and surges through the mind and heart of the intercessor. In this prayer by the apostle we have not only a sense of the depth of longing for the Christians, but also we are given a vision of God's plans for them.

Paul's prayer is very significant for you and me. Not only are we able to read it from the perspective of what Paul prayed for the Christians in A.D. 62, but we can also pray it with personal intensity for ourselves. A way to do this is to make it our own prayer by replacing the second person pronoun "you" with the first person "me." We will find this so exhilarating that we will want to use "you" again, focusing our concern on people who need all the glorious promises this prayer articulates so compellingly.

All of our inheritance that Paul has explained thus far in Ephesians is placed into the form of this prayer. It is as if the apostle said, "An explanation of the riches of your inheritance is not enough. You must experience them. My prayer now is that all I've said will be read to you and that you will live it."

I find it helpful to start at the conclusion of this prayer. It is even more glorious this way. In verse 20, Paul exclaims, "Now to Him who is able to do exceedingly abundantly above all that we ask or think, *according to the power that works in us*" (Eph. 3:20, italics mine). This is one of the apostle's "He is able" affirmations of the power of God in Christ.

Paul's confidence was not in his readers' ability, but in Christ's. The word "able" here is from the verb *dunamai,* which means literally "to have power." Christ has all power to do exceedingly abundantly above what we humanly would dare to ask. But we must be expectant and bold. "According to the power that works in us" means that the indwelling Christ engenders the picture of His potential for our lives. He works in us what He is willing to work out for us. He makes it possible for us to claim the superabundance offered to us. We would not dare to ask for it unless He formed in our minds the vision of the super-abundance He wants to release in our lives.

And what is this superlative work in us? It is exactly what Paul has just prayed for in his prayer in Eph. 3:14–19. In this light we can go back and review the prayer as the description of the power that works "in us."

COURAGE IN CIRCUMSTANCES

Paul first prayed for the Christians to have courage in difficult circumstances. He knew that they were in danger of losing heart. "Therefore I ask that you do not lose heart. . . . For this reason I bow my knees to the Father of our Lord Jesus Christ." Losing heart means the loss of verve, will, and determination. We speak of an athlete who has a heart to win or a person whose heart is really in his work. Then, too, we say, "I'm with you with all my heart," or "I've really got a heart for that cause."

The Christians' loss of heart prompted Paul to pray urgently and earnestly that the Lord would grant them "according to the riches of His glory, to be strengthened with might through His Spirit in the inner man, that Christ may dwell in your hearts by faith" (Eph. 3:16–17). Strength through power from Christ's indwelling Spirit is the secret of not losing heart.

THE NEED FOR COURAGE

I remember, for instance, a brilliant and successful young actor, who asked me to pray for him.

"What do you want me to pray?" I asked, hoping that he would reveal his deepest longing.

"Pray that I will have courage in a world of compromise," he answered intently.

We all echo this longing. We need courage for our own set of circumstances in a time when others are buckling under and losing heart.

What is courage? Here is an alliterative but accurate working definition. "Courage is a creative compulsion that is the composite of compelling convictions that calls us to consecrate all our capabilities and conscripts us in a cause that cannot be compromised."

Plutarch wrote, "Courage is not hazarding without fear, but being resolutely minded in a just cause." And an old Italian proverb suggests, "It is better to live one day as a lion than a hundred days as a sheep."

For us Christians, however, courage is a magnificent blend of the Lord's guidance in what we are to be and do. In other words, courage is Christ in our inner being—mind, emotions, and will.

We are all called to be overcomers. This means not only trying harder, but allowing Christ to work in and through us.

On the night before He was crucified, Christ said, "In the world you will have tribulation; but be of good cheer, I have overcome the world" (John 16:33). In the Greek, the word translated as "cheer" is "courage." It is something offered that we must willingly accept. A better rendering of Christ's words would be, "Take courage, I have overcome the world."

Christ spoke these words before the cross and the resurrection. He was sure of overcoming, which means victory. He was confident of the Father's victory and now dwells within us to give us the same confidence. It is *His* confidence, not something that we conjure up on our own to please Him.

We pray, "Lord, I can't make it without Your power. Give me the gift of courage!"

He responds, "I am in you, around you, above you, behind you, and go before you to show the way."

FOUR-DIMENSIONAL LOVE

Christ's love for us is amazing, indeed. Paul goes on in His prayer to claim the four dimensions of this love that is now to be rooted in the depth of our inner Spirit:

> that you, being rooted and grounded in love, may be able to comprehend with all the saints what is the width and length and depth and height—to know the love of Christ which passes knowledge; that you may be filled with all the fullness of God.
>
> (Eph. 3:17–19)

The first dimension of this love is width. This means it is inclusive. Regardless of what you have been, you have been elected, called, appointed, and set apart to belong to the Lord. Nothing can change this. You see, when His arms are outstretched He reaches around us and holds us with the tenderness and strength of His nail-pierced hands.

Does anything inside your spirit say to you in self-condemnation, "I have no right to this love after what I've been and said and done"? If so, know at this very moment that you are fully embraced by the same love that dwelt in Jesus of Nazareth who healed the sick with His touch. He is the Christ who wants to love you to the uttermost. Christ is always reaching out to you, embracing you with the wideness of His mercy.

Note that Christ's love is not only a wide love, but also a long love. Paul speaks of the length of it. By length, he means the inescapable quality of the Lord's love. There is no place where the Lord is not waiting for us. There is no distance we can go where He is unable to reach us. The arms that embrace us are long enough to reach us wherever we may have wandered. What the psalmist said about the ubiquity of the Lord is now our assurance in the ever-present Christ.

> Where can I go from Your Spirit?
> Or where can I flee from Your presence?
> If I ascend into heaven, You are there;
> If I make my bed in hell, behold, You are there.
> If I take the wings of the morning, And dwell in the

uttermost parts of the sea,
Even there Your hand shall lead me,
And Your right hand shall hold me.

(Ps. 139:7–10)

But Christ's love is not only long, it is deep. The cross plummets down to the bottom of our shame or loss. No abyss is deeper than His love can fathom. If you nurse a memory of a failure, of something you have done or have said or have been, of a broken relationship that you cannot mend, or of something that makes you ache inside, understand that you can sink to no depth in your self-condemnatory cauldron where He cannot reach you. He does not leave us to stew in the putrid juices of our negativism and self-judgment.

But Paul is not finished. He says that Christ's love reaches not only to the depths, but to the heights and beyond, to the unlimited possibilities of what we can be. He has so much more planned for us, for our relationships, for the person we are to become, for what we are to achieve and for the love we are to give, that it stretches our imagination beyond its limits. The height of His love rises beyond the farthest star, as well as sinking below the lowest hell. Whatever you can imagine for the rest of your life is nothing compared to what He has planned for you.

By ourselves we cannot imagine all that the Lord can do in and around us. Paul frankly admits this. Even though he prays that we should comprehend with the saints the width and length and depth and height of Christ's love, he also says that it is beyond our understanding. What he means is that it cannot be limited to our analysis of what is possible. We are offered nothing less than the fullness of God—Christ present with us and in us.

STRETCHING OUR VISION

Now we are back to where we began our review of Paul's prayer. What we are able to expect from Christ is dependent on the power He works in us. This power stretches our vision. Here is how mine was stretched.

I live in California in the Hollywood Hills. My home is above a reservoir named Lake Hollywood which serves a part of

Los Angeles. A tree-lined road about four miles long circles the reservoir. Many people exercise in the morning by running or walking along this beautiful, artificial lake. Whenever I drive by it on my way to an early morning breakfast meeting, I see people preparing for their run. To keep themselves from getting sore, they bend, stretch, and contort themselves into all sorts of shapes. It is amazing to see the different positions that people force themselves into in order to stretch the various muscles of their bodies.

One day, as I motored by the stretching crew, a question formed in my mind: *I wonder if these people have stretched their minds as much as the muscles of their bodies?* Before I could pat myself on the back with pride and self-satisfaction, the Lord answered me, "Lloyd, have *you* stretched your mind today?" So began a new practice for me of stretching my thinking.

I do perform certain bodily warm-up exercises which I begin as soon as I arise from bed. I stretch my legs and my back. I have also discovered a special way to stretch my neck. Because I am one of the stiff-necked people (physically and spiritually!), I twist my head to the right and left, then up and down, while I say "No" to the forces of evil, then a wonderful, extended "Yes" to the Lord, and finally repeat an affirmation that I can do all things through Christ who strengthens me.

I have composed a prayer, which is really my motto for supernatural living. I would like to share it with you so that you might join me in the adventure of living supernaturally.

> Lord, help me to see
> What You want me to be
> To expect the miracles of Your grace
> In all that I am called to face.

I must honestly admit that I have to rediscover the truth of my prayer many times over during the day. So often I find myself on the flat, horizontal level of working for God on my own strength. The Lord has to invade me repeatedly with the vision of what He can do by His power in and through me. Hour after hour I have to trade my dull, naturalistic view of a life of cause and effect for the Bible's supernaturalistic view of the intervention, inspiration, and instigation of the power of Christ.

Wherever I go, I find Christians living flat, horizontal lives. I see no verticality, no gusto in facing the challenges of life. Though we commit our lives to Christ and dutifully recite our prayers, we limit what we can do to our own intelligence and strength. Certainly, we are going to live forever. We believe in Jesus Christ as our Lord and Savior; therefore, our eternal life is assured. But what about Christ's promise, "I have come so that you might have life and live it abundantly" (John 10:10)?

Most of us live in a strenuous effort to be able for God. To glorify the God in whom we believe, we want to be faithful, obedient, caring, and loving. This will wear us out if we try to do it on our own strength. If it does not give us a heart attack or a nervous breakdown, it will create in us a dull, bland religiosity born of exhausted effort. None of these consequences is very attractive.

How exciting, then, to move from the commitment of the cause-and-effect naturalist to the life of the supernaturalist, to be aware that Christ enables us to envision what He wants to do and gives us the power to accomplish it.

DOWN-TO-EARTH APPLICATION

Let me apply this news to some of the basic, down-to-earth things that you and I go through every day. Consider the circumstances in which you live and the problems you face. Do you have a vision for each of these circumstances at work, in the neighborhood, in the church, or in the projects Christ has given you to do? Have you taken the time to allow Him to give you His vision, the power to believe it, and the freedom to trust Him completely to achieve it? Christ wants to stretch us far beyond what we can imagine.

Personally, I'm very thankful that Paul prostrated himself and allowed the Lord to pray through him the prayer we've considered in this chapter. Like the soldier who had to get down with Paul because of the handcuffs that bound him to the apostle, we can never pray feckless, furtive prayers again. We've heard what real prayer is like. And through it we can claim more than we ever imagined!

12

GLORY
IN
THE
CHURCH

The purpose of the church is no less than the chief end of man. It is to glorify God and *enjoy* Him forever and together.

Paul concludes his prayer for the Christians in Asia Minor with a doxology that clearly declares this purpose: "To Him be glory in the church by Christ Jesus throughout all ages, world without end. Amen" (Eph. 3:21).

The church exists to be the fellowship in which God is glorified. But note who does the glorifying. The New King James Version renders this verse in a way that suggests that it is Christ who glorifies the Father in the church. The Revised Standard Version is, "To him be glory in the church and in Christ Jesus together." This implies that the glory is given by the church and by Christ.

Whatever shade of meaning you choose, the compelling image is the same. Christ is in His church to glorify the Father through us. Glory means both manifestation and adoration. We behold glory and we give glory, and Christ enables us to do both. He is God's manifestation with us and in us, and the One who

101

motivates our praise. The Lord of the church is at the same time the glory of God in the church and the glorifier of God through the church.

This is a stirring and comforting thought for churches like yours and mine. We need a clear vision of what the church was meant to be. Churches, like individuals, become what they envision. Our churches move toward the image and goals we dream. We can move from what we are to what we are destined to be only if we see that purpose through Christ's eyes. Then we set our priorities and reorder our life together to effectively achieve what He created the church, and yes, our congregations, to accomplish.

Christ has called us to join Him in glorifying God as the church. Everything we do, say, plan, program, budget, and organize must work together for the ultimate purpose of glorifying and enjoying God.

MEANWHILE, BACK TO REALITY

You may have sighed to yourself, "Meanwhile, Lloyd, get back to reality, get back to the real world, get back into the church as I know it. What you're saying is lovely but you're not talking about the church today. That's so far from what my congregation is that I don't even know where to begin to grapple with what you've said."

But I want you to grapple with my words. There's been enough criticism of the church from within and without, and my intention in this chapter is not to add to the criticism.

Rather, we need a positive picture of what could happen in our churches if they were to allow Christ to be our glory and our instigation and inspiration for glorifying and enjoying God together.

Over the years, this picture of a local congregation in our time has been etched in my mind. I've tried to live the vision in the churches I've served together with adventuresome elders, deacons, and responsible laity. We've studied the Scriptures, prayed, and dreamed together. Then we've tried to structure the life of the parish according to the goals and priorities the Lord has revealed.

Any time I share with others the strategy He has given, I am painfully reminded of my own failures and unfinished agendas. But when I do present the strategy at leadership conferences or retreats, I usually receive requests for written copies of what I've shared. That's why I'd like to put in this chapter some thoughts about how there can be glory in the church. Some of my thoughts about the subject are scattered throughout previous books, but this pulls them all together.

I take it as a given that we all want our churches to be biblically authentic, Christ-centered, Spirit-empowered, life-changing, mission-oriented congregations. We move on together from that firm foundation.

QUADRADIMENSIONAL INVENTORY

There are four inventory questions I have asked of myself and church officers of the congregations I have served:

- What kind of people do we want to deploy in the world?
- What kind of church equips that kind of people?
- What kind of church offices (session, board, vestry) enable that kind of church?
- What kind of pastor(s) enliven that kind of church officers?

THE KIND OF PEOPLE WE WANT TO DEPLOY

The first question, what kind of people do we want to deploy in the world, is asked out of the biblical context that the church exists not for itself but for people outside it and the society in which it is placed. The church reaches out by creative evangelism and prophetic mission through the laity. We do not need to send people out into the world. They are there already. The challenge is to help them accept their calling and become effective.

To be in Christ is to be in ministry. We are called to be ministers. I never use the term minister for myself or the clergy of our church. All of Christ's people are ministers. We are all His

103

servants in relationships, at work, and in society. In our church, there's never a question whether anyone who believes in Christ is a minister. The question is: What kind of minister and to what extent are we living Christ's calling?

What kind of ministers do we want to deploy? In keeping with the theme of this book, we want *those who glorify and enjoy God.* We see this manifested through four qualities, irreducible ingredients of dynamic Christianity:

• A life-affirming, transforming experience of Christ's love, forgiveness, and power with an unreserved commitment to Him.

• An infilling of His Spirit and a life that reveals His character in the fruit of the Spirit—love, joy, peace, patience, kindness, goodness, faithfulness, gentleness, self-control—and the gifts of the Spirit, particularly faith, wisdom, knowledge, discernment, prayer, healing, and servanthood.

• An accepted call into the ministry of evangelism—loving, listening, serving, caring for individuals, with a readiness to share new life and introduce people to Christ.

• A specific involvement in mission in one of the suffering sores of our society.

Is this too much to ask of contemporary Christians in most congregations? Not at all. I think the problem is that we have expected far too little. In fact, when people are affirmed, they will rise to unprecedented heights because they know what's expected of them and are helped to reach these new heights.

In the Hollywood Presbyterian Church, our church leaders are absolutely clear about what we expect for our people. We have a vivid picture of the quality of people Christ is trying to produce. This image provides us with clear goals and priorities. We picture joyous, liberated, loving, courageous, servant people. We claim this from Christ, we pray persistently for it, and we work toward it. Essentially, Christ wants a laity through whom He can glorify God and extend the kingdom in the world.

WHAT KIND OF CHURCH?

What kind of church makes this kind of person possible? How can we pray and plan for Christ's glory in the church? We find it helpful to think of Christ's glory communicated through a quadrilateral church. The biblical calling of the church is:

- a worshiping congregation
- a healing community
- an equipping center
- a deployment commission.

I found it helpful to reorganize our church leaders into departments to both fulfill the purposes of the church and to give us congruity between function and form. In each department, we prayerfully seek the mind of Christ as to how He wants to glorify God through all the functions of His body. We try to remember what kind of people He wants us to place in the world, and what will best prepare them for their ministry. Our elders have taken prolonged retreats to set short- and long-range goals that reflect Christ's answers to these questions for our church life.

WORSHIPING CONGREGATION

As a worshiping congregation, the saints gather around Christ to glorify God through worship which is Christ-inspired and Christ-guided. He glorifies the Father through us as we sing praise, either led by the choir or in congregational singing. Since confession means "to say after," we allow Christ to help us confess those things that stand between us and our ability to worship God.

Thanksgiving for Christ's forgiveness following our confession breaks forth in joyous response. Then, with Christ in the midst of our worship, we pray our prayers of intercession and supplication in the power of His name, the name that reaches the Father's heart and conquers the forces of evil. Our corporate prayers of dedication are for the ministry of each member and for our witness together as a congregation.

Refocusing the purpose of worship has led us to a renewed understanding of the role of preaching. We have taken Rom. 15:29 as our guide. Writing to the Christians in Rome, Paul said, "But I know that when I come to you, I shall come in the fullness of the blessing of the gospel of Christ." When we preach, we are to come to people with the gospel of Christ. The gospel is His life, message, and power for all of our existence. We approach life's problems with the assurance of His blessing—the strength and courage to live amid the pressures, suffering, and frustrations of contemporary life. And the fullness of Christ's indwelling Spirit is the secret of living the exhilarating call to discipleship.

We call this "quadraphonic preaching." We believe that the Bible is the inspired, authoritative Word of God; that Christ is the center of the proclamation of redemption, conversion, and new life; that the plumb line of the gospel is lowered to establish our call to justice and social responsibility; and that the baptism and repeated infilling of the Spirit is essential for a Christ-empowered life. We believe Christ is calling us to biblical, evangelical, socially responsible, Spirit-filled preaching. Our hope is that on any Sunday, people can receive what they would find in a Bible church, an evangelical church, a social action church and a charismatic church—all rolled into one; the whole gospel for all the people.

Prayerful reevaluation of the church as a worshiping congregation has enabled us to sense where people are as they come to worship and where Christ wants them to be by the conclusion of the service.

We believe our church is called to minister to four groups: the outside-outsider, who is outside of Christ and outside of fellowship; the inside-outsider, who is inside of Christ but has not yet made a commitment to be part of the body of Christ; the outsider-insider, religious people in the membership who need a transforming experience of Christ and an infilling of His Spirit; and, the insider-insider, who is both in Christ and in the church, but who needs encouragement and training to live with boldness and courage.

Our conviction is that we cannot feed the hungry in all four groups without a consistent exposition of the Scriptures, which weekly presents the "fullness of the blessing of the gospel of Christ."

106

An aspect of our renewal experience is the secret of listening. Yearly we survey the deepest needs and most urgent questions of our people. I take these with me on my summer study leave and use them as I plan the sermons for the next year. As I study, I feel the hurts and hopes of my people as the Lord presses them onto my heart.

I think of the old adage: "There is nothing so foolish as the answer to an unasked question or a solution to an unexpressed problem." I like to paraphrase it to, "There is nothing so powerful as a Christ-inspired answer or solution in an exposition of a Bible verse or passage when it touches people's raw nerves and aching needs."

After the sermons for the next year are outlined with title, text, and an explanation of the theme and progression of the message, then our director of music plans all the anthems, responses, hymns, and contemporary congregational songs around the central theme of each week's exposition. This allows us to use a variety of music and frees us to be guided by Christ in innovative ways of glorifying and enjoying God in worship.

We have found that it's the predictable sameness that often makes worship dull and bland. Christ is the same yesterday, today, and forever, but the many ways He leads us to glorify with gladness is constantly invigorated by fresh inspiration.

In leading worship we keep three sayings before us. One is the urgent appeal of the Greeks to Philip in Jerusalem during the last days of Jesus' ministry, "Sir, we want to see Jesus!" The second is Richard Baxter's reminder, "I preach as a dying man to dying men and women as if never to preach again." And thirdly, on the door leading from the robing room into the sanctuary, the words, "In the name of Jesus, put the arms of your heart around the congregation." All three exhortations infuse great enthusiasm to our opening call to worship, "The Living Christ is here—let us glorify and enjoy God together!"

HEALING COMMUNITY

The church is also called to be a healing community. Salvation brings healing and wholeness in the basic relationships of our life —with God; with ourselves, within our minds, emotions, and bodies; with others; and with our world. Christ is our Healer. He seeks to glorify the Father by mediating the power of His Spirit's healing for our spiritual, psychological, physical, and interpersonal needs.

Several years ago, the elders of my church sought the guidance of Christ for a healing ministry. We were convinced that Christ desires to do through the church today what He did through the apostles in the Book of Acts. The spiritual gift of praying for healing is for now as much as it was for then.

Throughout those years, we have grown aware of our calling to pray for healing in one another's lives as a natural part of our congregation. This happens informally two by two as we share needs in classes; before, during, and after meetings; and on the phone and whenever a distress signal is given by one of the saints. In addition, we have other expressions of the healing ministry of the church.

At the conclusion of our worship services, an invitation is given for people to come forward to the front of the sanctuary to kneel and pray with the elders. This is a part of the dedication portion of the worship service before the benediction, and often it continues long afterward.

The invitation is for people to receive Christ as Savior and Lord, unite with the church, or to pray for the healing of needs. Each week people stream forward to commit their hurts and hopes to Christ and claim His healing power. Lives are changed, miracles happen, and people are set free of their anxiety and the burden of carrying their problems alone.

While we pray for specific healing of needs, we also pray and affirm the healing professions. Some of the elders in the prayer ministry are physicians, psychologists, and psychiatrists.

Another healing focus is within our small group program. We are encouraged to cluster together throughout the community in groups of no more than twelve. The purpose of these groups is to study the Bible, share needs, and pray for one another. There are groups of singles, couples, teenagers, college and young adults, as well as special groups for business, entertainment, and professional people.

Also, a crucial expression of our healing ministry is through

the work of our Care and Counseling Department which provides pastoral counseling and training of lay counselors. We also have a Creative Counseling Center staffed by a psychiatrist and several psychologists to help meet the more intricate needs within the congregation.

EQUIPPING CENTER

In Eph. 4:12 Paul declares that the leadership of the church is appointed "for the equipping of the saints for ministry, for the edifying of the body of Christ." The church is called to be an equipping center for training every member for his or her ministry of living out the faith, personal witness and evangelism, and specific mission to heal human suffering.

The church as an equipping center involves both Inquirers groups for training new Christians and candidates for membership and in the ongoing program of classes to equip people for their ministries. I like to think of the church as a seminary for lay ministers.

I am profoundly moved each time our elders meet with an Inquirers group of candidates for membership. Many are new Christians, some are reaffirming their faith, and others are transferring their membership.

The exciting thing to me is the variety of types of people and the unique way Christ has worked in their lives—loving them, transforming them into new people, and conscripting them into the ministry. After ten weeks of training, they appear before the Session to share what Christ means to them, the facet of the church's equipping program in which they intend to be involved, and the focus of their ministry.

Everything we do in the church should be a part of the total equipping program. However, it is in the church school classes, week-day courses, retreats and conferences that the comprehensive training for ministry is accomplished. We try to keep before us the kind of people we want to deploy in the world, and this helps us set the direction of the curriculum. Our goal is spiritual formation through study of the Scriptures, prayer, theology, ethics and holy living, and practical training in the skills of lay ministry.

DEPLOYMENT COMMISSION

The glory of Christ is a person filled with His Spirit and engaged in evangelism and mission. The role of the church is to launch people in their particular area of calling.

When a church deploys, or commissions, someone, we send that person on an assignment.

Our Missions and Deployment Department, besides guiding our financial giving to local, national, and world mission programs, actively evaluates the needs of our community and deploys our people in active ministry in those needs.

An ebb and flow takes place within the church as we deploy members. People are encouraged to find the need Christ wants them to fill, and then we help them find others who share that concern. We form a task force to study the problem, then move toward action and provide mutual support for one another. Sometimes other needs are defined by the Mission and Deployment Department staff who form a task force and recruit members to fill the task force. These task forces confront the various needs in our community, such as, hunger, the homeless, runaway children from all over the nation who gravitate to Hollywood, pornography, women and child abuse, substance abuse, the City-Dweller program ministering to community youth and family needs, AIDS, catastrophic illness, and the complicated issues of abortion and homosexuality.

The exciting thing is that there's no limit to either the number of directions or different directions these mission task forces can take.

Now we are ready to consider briefly the church offices needed to enable this kind of church. Then, finally, we'll examine what kind of pastor can enliven dynamic church officers.

THE CHURCH IN MINIATURE

We think of our Session, made up of all the elders, as a church in miniature. (I'll leave it to you, the reader, to change the name of the key officers in your church—whoever is responsible to shape the goals and program of the parish.) We believe that the quality of life experienced by our Session directly determines the spiritual dynamism of our church as a whole. We think of it this way: our

110

church will move forward only as fast and far as the elders have experienced Christ's glory together.

Some spiritual laws are at work within our Session: Nothing can happen *through* us which has not happened *to* us; we can reproduce only what we are in the process of rediscovering for ourselves; and our own spiritual growth determines the extent to which we can help others mature.

It is crucial to elect leaders who are vitally alive in Christ, are growing in discipleship, and are wide open to His supernatural power to lead a supernatural church. They must be people who are secure in their sainthood, filled with the Spirit, equipped with the gifts of the Spirit, and free in the Spirit. *There must be undeniable evidence that these leaders enjoy and glorify God.* To state the obvious, if we want to deploy in the world people who are biblically rooted, Christ-centered, Spirit-empowered, evangelism-motivated, and missions-oriented, then we need lay leaders who are active in ministry themselves.

A good question to ask is: "If the whole church were a projection of the spirituality of a candidate for church leadership, what kind of church would it be?" Likewise, church leaders need to ask themselves the same question: "What is my boldest dream for my church? Am I living what I long for the whole church to be?"

Equally important is how elders perceive the work of the Session. If the leadership group is only a board to weigh facts and set policies, then the church is in trouble.

The Session is to be the beloved community gathered around Christ to be to each other His love, forgiveness, vision, and hope. This commitment requires as much time in prayer and fellowship as is spent doing the business of the church. Leaders must be a tightly knit, unified body of believers whose sole goal is to discover Christ's maximum plan for a parish, to live that in miniature together, and then to communicate this vision to the whole congregation.

Let's look at some basic examples. Every Christian should be reproductive—are the elders leading people to Christ? No Christian should be without a mission—are the elders personally in mission? Tithing is the absolute minimum, biblical standard for giving—do the elders exemplify this biblical mandate? When the elders are these kind of disciples, there will be no limit to how Christ will glorify the Father in a church.

To begin this adventure in our churches, we need to start from where we are. Making a start requires a clear focus of what the church is called to be and do, which takes honesty, humility, and a commitment to live our lives and lead our churches according to Christ's mandate and by His supernatural power.

ENLIVENED BY THE PASTOR

The pastor is pivotal. He or she is the one called by Christ to preach what He has done, to prophesy what He has promised to do, to communicate personally what He is ready to do, and to program so that it will be done.

Tall order for a pastor? Yes, but the pastor is not called to do it alone. Christ is the Senior Shepherd. He is Lord of the church. And He is ready to use pastors who will put Him first in their lives and allow Him to use him or her as a channel for the flow of His vision. The pastor is not the hope of the church but the one whose primary calling is to spend the time required in studying the Scriptures and prayer until the vision flames in his or her mind and heart. This personal time with the Lord must be in addition to time spent in preparation to preach.

Prophetic preaching is strategic in the renewal of the church. Prophecy is vividly forthtelling the truth—forcefully, irresistibly, winsomely. If there's no fire in the pulpit there's little chance of the church being on fire. The great need for the church is for biblical exposition that's both revelational and relational. The Scriptures must be explained, but also illustrated with contemporary stories about how the truth can be lived today.

There also needs to be that moment in every message when the preacher leans into conversation and with one-to-one intensity says, "Allow me to share what this means to me personally." Then the personal joy, excitement, pain, and vulnerability thunder through. It is from the pulpit that the fourfold calling of every Christian and the fourfold purpose of the church must be communicated.

I believe there is no way to do this kind of preaching without the equivalent of two ten-hour days a week. Some preachers prefer to put that into a solid block of two successive days; others would rather spread it out over five four-hour periods. Some who are the primary preachers on a multiple pastoral staff may have the privilege of even greater time for sermon preparation, but no preacher of any church large or small can afford less than twenty hours.

It's in the pastoral role that the personal relationships with church officers are developed into friendships. One-to-one and in small clusters the vision proclaimed from the pulpit must be grappled with and talked through. The Lord wants an adventuresome band of friends through whom He can impart the vision. Since a church will move no faster or further than the elders are living individually and together, the pastor must begin with them and never let up.

In the ambience of affirmation, trust, and openness the Session becomes a fellowship of friends, covenant brothers and sisters with whom the inventory questions about where the church is going can be asked and answered together.

The role of the pastor as programmer is also strategic. Christ *does* equip leaders with gifts to be strategists. But we've all learned repeatedly that people can support only what they've shared in envisioning and developing. So, the pastor is one of a team of elders who seek Christ's guidance in five-, three-, and one-year plans. Through His guidance, new programs are hammered out until everyone agrees to them and commits to them. Papers on a congregation's stand on issues must be written so the session can support a particular direction. And, like a family that feels the strength of a mother and father who are of one mind, so, too, a congregation will sense the impact of unified direction from the church officers.

One further word about pastors who foster glory in the church. Most of them have a covenant group outside their churches in which, on a regular basis, they can go to receive healing and renewed strength. The demands of leading a parish are enervating, with great potential for disappointment and discouragement, and the very real possibility of physical and spiritual burnout. The pastor needs a place where he or she can go while bruised and bleeding, exhausted and depleted, and be listened to and prayed for. Within this covenant group the pastor's vision can be recaptured and new hope engendered.

Christ is not finished with His church. It's His chosen instrument on earth through which He intends to glorify the Father. We are uniquely called, distinctly different, and sublimely blessed to be the church, those who "enjoy Him forever."

"To God be glory in the church by Christ Jesus throughout all ages, world without end. Amen."

13

BEING
A
SPIRITUAL
SPENDTHRIFT

A Scotswoman described her husband's money management problems in a colorful way: "'e's a blooming spendthrift. A real prodigal. Money gushes through his 'ands like a raging river. It's as if 'e's got a source that could never be diminished."

In further conversation with this woman, I discovered that her husband's problem was made up of three different elements. First, he was a hopelessly optimistic gambler; second, he was a big spender; and last, he was a soft touch for anyone who asked him for anything.

With this volatile, explosive combination you can imagine the problems this couple had within their marriage and their home. Yet, as I reflected on what this woman had said about her husband, I deeply longed to become a spendthrift of a different kind —a spiritual spendthrift.

A spendthrift, you know, is one who uses money with excessive freedom. And a prodigal, to use the true meaning of the word, is one who is lavish, excessive, and unrestrained.

I thought, *I would love to be able to enjoy the spiritual resources of God as a river rushing through me.* I remembered again Jesus'

We know the depth from which we have been raised, and we know the heights to which the Lord intends us to go. Thus, to be humble is to glorify the Lord in the use of the talents and gifts He has given us. We take no credit ourselves for these talents and gifts. We use them with freedom and abandonment and give glory to the Lord.

The posture of the Christian walk is characterized by receptivity. A humble person is gratefully receptive to what the Lord has to give. A person who is not humble thinks that he has made a success of himself and that he knows everything. Not so the Christian. The longer we live as Christians, the more we realize what we have to learn and discover. We know we have only begun to receive what the Lord has to pour out.

How few humble Christians we know! How seldom are we humble. So quickly we become satisfied with life and begin to glorify ourselves rather than the Lord. We end up in a dull, dead eddy instead of in the mainstream of His power.

GENTLENESS

The second step in the walk of the Christian is *gentleness*. This is a translation of the word "meekness," which is *praotes* in Greek.

In Aristotle's explanation of meekness it means the distinction between too much anger and too little anger. It expresses the middle ground between overindulgence and underindulgence. Meekness is power that is channeled, under control.

Jesus Christ is the ultimate example of meekness.

As He walked among people He was humble because He knew He could be a spiritual spendthrift. His resources had no limit. Lavishly He drew on the grace of God. He knew how to channel God's power.

Christ's persecutors seized Him, lashed His back, stretched Him out on a cross, and yet He remained a spendthrift. "Father," He prayed, "forgive them, for they know not what they do."

"We did away with Him!" His persecutors shouted.

But He returned in the ubiquitous power of the Spirit.

The disciples said triumphantly, "He's unloosed on the world. There is no stopping Him now!"

Now the Spendthrift arrives and recruits spendthrifts who are meek enough to come under His control. Such are the meek.

LONG-SUFFERING

Our next step is *long-suffering,* which also means patience. A Christian who is Christly knows the shortness of time and the length of eternity. Because Christ extended grace to him, he is willing and able to extend grace to those around him. We are compassionate when others fail because Christ was compassionate when we failed. We are gentle to those who are hurting because Christ was gentle when we hurt. When we look into another's heart with Christ's eyes, we become spendthrifts in regard to his feelings, his pain, and his anguish.

We can only do this if we have experienced the limitless supply of Christ's love. We cannot love people who are difficult to love and forgive those who have hurt us unless we recognize that the more love and forgiveness we give away, the more we will be given.

The wonderful thing about a spiritual spendthrift is that he knows he cannot outgive Christ. The more he gives away, the more the Lord blesses. The more abandoned, the more lavish, and the more unqualified the love, the more the Lord gives. We give God pleasure when we give away His love. And we enjoy Him in His pleasure with us.

Constantly, our patience has to be replenished. I am not naturally a patient person. My whole being moves at high speed the minute my feet hit the floor in the morning. As the day goes on, I go faster and faster. By eleven o'clock at night I am impatient with myself and the entire world.

"Lord," I pray, "slow me down so that I can live at Your pace, think Your thoughts and be more understanding of other people."

Then, in my fast-moving race through life, sometimes I trip and fall flat on my face. My nose gets bruised and I hurt. As I pull myself up and say, "Lord, I fell," He answers, "Well, maybe the bruise on the end of your nose can help you understand what other people are going through. And be more patient."

Suddenly, patience, *makrothumia,* begins to flow, and a renewed Christliness comes.

FORBEARANCE

The fourth element of the Christly walk is *forbearance.* The Greek word used here by Paul is from the verb *anecho,* to hold up. It implies uplifting, or carrying. The noun is *anoche,* which means to hold back and relates to holding back judgment for punishment. To lift people up and help carry their burdens is a vital part of our calling. We can do it only if we have been uplifted by Christ and remember how He forgave and encouraged us when we were down.

RECONCILIATION

The fifth triumphant step in our walk is the peace that comes from abiding in Christ. This is the *reconciliation* that Christ places within us. Peace between people results from forgiveness. In order to be forgiving, we have to be forgiven consistently, over and over again. When we are at peace, the wonderful quality of the presence of Christ invades the discord and hurt of our relationships and brings healing.

Everything Paul says has the purpose of making us Christly in our relationships. Our position is the grace of God. Our posture is to exhibit these five qualities of love: humility, gentleness, long-suffering, forbearance, and reconciliation.

So, how are you walking?

JUST LOVELY WORDS?

"But what good are all these lovely words about love?" you ask. "What I need is a handle that will let me get a hold of it."

This is the secret: the Father who reigns over all is present with us in the power of Jesus Christ. His Spirit enters into us and gives us the power to be like Himself. If you think you can be a Christlike person on your own, you cannot. It's a miracle He Himself does in us.

Now here's the litmus test: Have you ever asked to be made Christly? We have to want this more than anything else.

In Galatians, Paul writes, "If we live in the Spirit, let us also walk in the Spirit" (Gal. 5:25). When we take each step with the humble, receptive openness and commitment to be Christlike to others, God's limitless power is released. An inner walking pace begins: the step and the power, the step and the power.

I want to ask you to join with me in being a spiritual, prodigal spendthrift. Are you willing to try? Think what could happen in your home, your marriage, your friendships, and where you work. Everything could be different because *you* are different.

As the verse in the old hymn "Trust and Obey" says:

> When we walk with the Lord
> In the light of His Word,
> Oh, what glory He sheds on the way.
> When we do His good will,
> He abides with us still,
> And with all who will trust and obey.

14

GIFTS
FOR
THE
GIFTED

Gifts for the gifted. I've worded this phrase very carefully. In four words it expresses what God does to enable us to enjoy Him and how He equips us to rejoice in serving Him. The phrase also describes the essence of the New Testament truth about primary gifts and spiritual gifts. There is great interest today in spiritual gifts, accompanied by an equal amount of confusion and misunderstanding. My purpose in this chapter is to heighten your interest in these gifts and to clear up any of the misunderstandings that you might have about them.

In Eph. 4:7–12, Paul tells us that Christ makes us gifted people and offers us gifts. Let's discuss both as we consider Paul's dramatic description of the reigning Lord of the church. "But to each one of us grace was given according to the measure of Christ's gift. Therefore He says: 'When He ascended on high, He led captivity captive, and gave gifts to men.'"

In glorifying Christ as the victorious Lord the apostle paraphrases Ps. 68:18. The psalm itself paints a picture of a returning victor with his captives in his train. It is the description of a king's triumphant entry into Jerusalem. His captives are in chains, staggering behind him. The conquering hero has taken gifts from his captives as spoil to bring to the Holy City.

Careful observation reveals that Paul, receiving the inspiration from Christ Himself ("Therefore *He* says"), has reworded the psalm. The picture of the conquering hero is now remarkably different. He has not wrenched gifts as spoil from the captives but gives gifts to them!

The message is that Christ is the conquering hero who has now transformed our captivity in the bondage to sin and self-centeredness into a captivating allegiance to Him. Instead of demanding gifts from us, He is the unstintingly generous *giver* of gifts.

Paul's central message is reiterated. God has made Christ the reigning Lord of the church and the One through whom people are both gifted and receive gifts.

YOU ARE A GIFTED PERSON

You and I have been elected, chosen and called to be gifted people. Notice that I didn't say talented. In our culture we describe highly talented people as gifted. Certainly all our abilities are divine endowments. But I'm using the term "gifted" in a very different way. A gifted person is one who has been given the basic gifts of grace, salvation, faith, and the indwelling Spirit of Christ.

Paul gives a stirring summary of our giftedness in Eph. 2:8–9, "For by grace you have been saved through faith, and that not of yourselves; it is a gift of God, not of works lest anyone should boast. For we are His workmanship created in Christ Jesus for good works which God has prepared beforehand that we should walk in them."

Grace is the gift of Christ, faith is a gift to believe in Christ, and salvation is a gift given to live in Christ now and forever. This is our inheritance. When we claim it we become gifted people, as Paul writes: "And to each one of us grace was given according to the measure of Christ's gift" (4:7). The word measure, *metron*, means a determined extent or portion. Here it means that our gift of grace is measured and determined by the will of Christ. The Father is the ultimate source of grace. The Son is both the focus and facilitator of this grace in our hearts and minds.

GIFTED FOR GIFTS

Spiritual gifts are given to the gifted. Through the Spirit, Christ wants to give us gifts to equip us for our ministry. Every Christian has been called into the ministry of Christ. To be in Christ is to be in ministry. We all have a ministry to people: to communicate grace, to introduce them to Christ, and to care for their spiritual, physical, emotional, interpersonal, and social needs. Our mission in life is people, their salvation and their total well-being. Thus we stand on a two-legged ministry of personal evangelism and social responsibility to improve anything in our society that debilitates, demeans, or dehumanizes people. Private piety and social irresponsibility have no place in the life of a Christian. To tolerate either in our lives is to deny our Lord and our own giftedness. I stress this again because many Christians have not accepted the call into ministry and mission given to *every* Christian.

What's equally tragic is that many have not realized or accepted the spiritual gifts for their ministry. They are trying to do their ministry of evangelism and mission on human talent alone. The reasons are varied. Some Christians are arrogant enough to think they can pull off a ministry on their own with their own intelligence, skill, and personality. The primary cause is lack of understanding of what God offers us for our ministry. Finally, some unbiblical teachings about spiritual gifts dominate the thinking of many groups of Christians.

Let's look first at the spiritual gifts offered to us by reviewing one of the most detailed lists in the New Testament—in 1 Corinthians 12.

The gift of *wisdom* is the supernatural power to know the mind of Christ—His will, plan and purpose—for ourselves, other people, and circumstances.

Through the gift of *knowledge* God gives us needed information about practical situations and relationships. We are given x-ray vision into people, their needs, and what the Lord wants us to say or do.

Faith as a spiritual gift is not the primary faith by which we respond to the gospel and become Christians, but the confident trust that the Lord can and will do what He has revealed by

125

wisdom and knowledge. This gift of faith gives us expectancy, boldness, and courage to claim the Lord's promise.

The gift of *healing* responds to the manifold needs of people. Christ is the source of all healing of the body, mind, and spirit. God's healing restores us to the wholeness for which we were created. In times of sickness, God entrusts a special endowment to His people to envision wholeness and claim it. He also blesses the professional practice of medicine and psychiatry and calls us to undergird with prayer the work of these professionals.

The gift of *discernment* enables us to detect the power of evil. It allows us to determine whether something is part of Satan's diabolical influence or whether it is the Spirit of the Lord at work. This is a crucial gift when so many beguiling people, ideas and causes parade themselves as authentic when they may in fact be Satan's tools. With the gift of discernment we know the difference.

Prophecy is not necessarily foretelling, but forth-telling. It's to be in such a profound communion with the Lord so as to speak forth what He's saying in a particular circumstance. Specific prophecies must always be weighed in the biblical balance and never replace God's ultimate revelation in Scripture. In fact, prophetic messages usually reiterate biblical truths needed in a given situation.

The gift of *tongues* is perhaps the most controversial gift of the Spirit. It is speaking in a divinely inspired language which may be unlike any of the languages of humankind. Properly used, it can supersede the reticence of human language to speak to the church gathered for praise and supplication. At the same time, the Lord gives the gift of *interpretation* by which one can speak forth to people in their natural language that which has been communicated in tongues.

Though not mentioned in Paul's list in 1 Corinthians 12, the gift of *praying in tongues* is what is called "praying in the Spirit." This happens when a person who is praying ascends into union with the Spirit and prays with a supernatural language. Often, at a subsequent moment, the person is given the power to interpret what the Spirit has prayed in an unknown language. Guidance or inspiration is given beyond what a person could discover by human reason.

Paul goes on to assert in 1 Corinthians 13 that the gift of *love* is the highest and most needed of the spiritual gifts. It is the gift to be able to love with the inspiration and intention of the Lord Himself. The gift of love is not human affection or good will felt intensely, but the Spirit of love using us as a channel to express His grace to another person or group.

Romans 12 gives us a further list of gifts with an emphasis on the equipment of the Spirit for our relationships. "Having then gifts differing according to the grace that is given to us, let us use them" (v. 6). Paul then lists the gifts for helping people: prophecy, service, exhortation, giving, leadership, teaching, showing mercy, and hospitality.

THE HELPER JESUS GIVES US

The gifts of the Spirit specifically equip Christians to be able to fulfill Jesus' promise to continue His ministry.

> Most assuredly, I say to you, he who believes in Me, the works that I do he will do also; and greater works than these he will do, because I go to My Father. And whatever you ask in My name, that I will do, that the Father may be glorified in the Son. If you ask anything in My name, I will do it. If you love Me, keep My commandments. And I will pray the Father, and He will give you another Helper, that He may abide with you forever. . . . I will not leave you orphans; I will come to you.
>
> (*John 14:12–18*)

Jesus spoke these words on the night before the crucifixion. The greater work of Jesus that we are to do is to lead men and women to Him. Jesus spoke of the Holy Spirit as "another helper," another like Jesus Himself. As reigning Lord of the church, He is the appointed administrator of the infilling of the Spirit in His people. Through the Spirit, Jesus continues His ministry in us. We are equipped to love, forgive, care, heal, serve, teach, do miracles, discern and speak truth, and liberate the captives, just as Jesus did, in order to accomplish the greater work of leading people to Him and helping them to become mature in Him.

Even this very brief review of the spiritual gifts and their purpose shows us the immense divine power available to us. Like any of the resources of the Lord, they must be used for His glory and not in the service of self-aggrandizement.

SITUATIONAL GIFTS

The spiritual gifts are given for specific needs in particular situations. God gives us the exact gift we need to minister in a particular circumstance. Those who know and enjoy God are able to receive the appropriate gift to facilitate God's work at a given moment. We never possess the gifts as permanent endowments. The Holy Spirit is like a tool chest filled with many different kinds of equipment. When we are open to love and service, the Spirit has certain gifts as tools and entrusts their use to us. Once we have used the tool, we no longer possess it. But we continue to be filled with the tool-giver—the Holy Spirit Himself. As we continue in ministry, we need different gifts to meet the changing challenges.

CONFUSION ABOUT THE GIFTS

Now we are able to confront the immense misunderstanding about spiritual gifts today.

First, there is confusion about the meaning of being gifted and receiving gifts. Often we speak of a person who has exercised one of the gifts consistently as one permanently gifted with that gift. We may refer to someone as a healer, prophet, teacher, or worker of miracles. This has two debilitating effects: it often keeps the person from being open to using other spiritual tools from the tool chest, and it can lead a person away from moment-by-moment dependence on the Holy Spirit. We focus our spirituality around one gift and take pride in having that gift. Often this pride is manifested by subtly judging others who do not have this gift.

Sadly, the gift of speaking in tongues has been identified as the clearest sign that a person is filled with the Spirit. As liberating and moving as the gift of tongues can be, it's neither the only gift nor a superior gift.

The motto I like is—All the gifts for all the people for all different opportunities of ministry.

Another misunderstanding of spiritual gifts centers on the belief that some of them were given only for the apostolic age.

Those with this point of view assert that the dramatic "sign" gifts, such as healing or tongues, were given during the first century for the establishment and expansion of the church and are no longer operating today. The only gifts given now, these people argue, are basic gifts of grace, faith, salvation, and sanctification, as well as the more "mundane" gifts, such as teaching and service.

But, in fact, all gifts are "sign" gifts—signs of the power of the Spirit. And all the gifts are for service, for building up the body of Christ. The Book of Acts shows us normative Christianity: all gifts functioning by the power of the Spirit for the growth of the church. The church today is meant to be the new chapter in the Book of Acts.

A further misapprehension is created by thinking of a particular calling in the church as a spiritual gift. We speak incorrectly of a person called into a certain ministry as having the gift of evangelism, preaching, teaching, pastoral care, or administration. To be sure, Christ does give apostles, prophets, evangelists, and pastor-teachers to the church, as our passage states (Eph. 4:11–12). A prophet would regularly receive specific gifts of prophecy, but he or she would not "have the gift." A prophet has been called by God into an avenue of ministry. But this calling is not the same as a spiritual gift.

Church leaders are given by Christ for equipping and edifying the church. The word "equip" means to mend and heal, as well as to outfit with the tools necessary to accomplish a task. The Greek word for "equip" was used to describe both the mending of nets and, in the practice of medicine, mending of the brokenness of health in the body. "Edifying" was closely related to "equip." It means the act of building and is used figuratively by the apostle for the promotion of spiritual upbuilding of the believer.

For their challenging and demanding calling, leaders in the church need all the gifts. For example, if you are called to preach, you must constantly depend on the Spirit's gifts of love, wisdom, knowledge, faith, prophecy, healing and working of miracles if your preaching is to have any impact toward mending and upbuilding the saints.

I would not dare to step into the pulpit of my church without personal prayer for these gifts and without the regular laying on of hands in prayer by the elders in our 9:00 A.M. weekly prayer time before our two Sunday morning worship services. I'm thankful for the talents, education, training, and experience the Lord has entrusted to me, but I am gifted to preach only when I ask and open myself up for the flow of gifts. And I can never take it for granted that if I was given gifts last week, I now possess them permanently for however many more years the Lord calls me to preach. The same goes for any of the other callings of leadership in the church. We are channels of the gifts, not reservoirs in which to store them.

The same is true for the laity. If you are called into personal evangelism as a member of a church, then you are given gifts— moment by moment, encounter by encounter—for your calling. If you are called to be an elder or deacon or vestryperson, your talents of leadership are recognized apart from the spiritual gifts you will need with which to function on a merely human level.

Take, for example, a skilled, talented executive. You will have experience in management, fiscal affairs, personnel, and planning. These capabilities will certainly be maximized by the Spirit in leading the church. But what you need most are the gifts of the Spirit for courageous, bold, and exciting spiritual leadership of the church.

Dr. Jack Kerr, professor of management at the University of Southern California, is an excellent example of this. He trains students in the skills of running an organization. In Jack's calling as an elder, he uses all his education to help in the administration of the church, but he doesn't stop here. He is consistently open to the gifts of the Spirit for purposes of personal evangelism, mission, leading Bible study groups, and participating with the other elders in our church's ministry of healing at the conclusion of our worship services. Jack is not locked into using any one gift.

Inez Smith would exemplify the same truth. She served for years as the administrative assistant to Dr. David Hubbard, president of Fuller Theological Seminary. She puts her broad experience into practice on our personnel committee, however. Meeting after meeting, decision by decision, Inez asks for and receives the spiritual gifts of wisdom, knowledge, and discernment. She's never locked into any one gift. Wherever the Lord leads her in the leadership of the Body of Christ, she's ready to listen, counsel,

130

and pray for people with a fresh inflow of the gifts of healing and expectancy for the miracles the Lord performs.

In all our opportunities for ministry, we serve a sovereign Lord who is in control. He will decide what gift we need and when we need it. Our responsibilities are to seek first the kingdom, to seek to equip and edify others in the church and in our evangelism, and to expect that we will be divinely empowered by whatever gift is needed in a situation.

SEEK TO SERVE

So often we hear the admonition that we should seek the Giver and not the gifts. That's not good advice. We've already been found by the Giver of life. By grace He's made us gifted people. Now we should seek the gifts so that we can serve Him and others. We have the privilege of praying for and receiving whatever spiritual gifts the Lord will give us to minister with supernatural power.

Gifts to the gifted. We are gifted by the Lord's choice. We choose to receive His spiritual gifts. Not only are we to seek constant, renewed fellowship with the Lord, but also the gifts of His Spirit. We are offered the fullness of Christ.

15

THE
FULLNESS
OF
CHRIST

Oliver Cromwell had a motto which spurred him on in his growth as a Christian. It was written in Latin and placed in his pocket Bible. *Oui cessat esse melior cessat esse bonus* — "He who ceases to be better ceases to be good."

Before you type this out to put in your Bible or on a plaque for your desk to spur you on to greater efforts toward self-improvement, however, let me warn you that it will cause one of the greatest struggles of your life. Pithy statements like this can be dangerous. I've tried to press myself into self-improvement programs for years, using this motto and thousands of others as a motivation.

And the result? Frustration! I did not get better "every day in every way." Even though I set high goals for what I wanted to do and be as a Christian, I found that my best efforts soon dwindled and I'd be back where I started. The same old patterns, habits, and personality would return. Most of all, the same old "I" inside me came back. Talk about struggles—this was the biggest struggle!

At the same time, Paul's words mocked me. His bold promises about growing in Christ convicted me. I remember reading the verse from Ephesians saying that our rebirth-right as Christians is to "come to the unity of the faith and the knowledge of the Son of God, to a perfect man, to the measure of the stature of the fullness of Christ" (Eph. 4:13).

A CHALLENGING IMAGE

The fullness of Christ? This glorious image challenged me. How could I know this? Intuitively, I sensed that it contained the secret of growth in the Christian life. Though I wanted this fullness, my searching efforts and attempted discipline left me more disquieted. I began a pilgrimage of the soul, a quest to discover what Paul meant and how I could realize it.

The purpose of this chapter and the next is to share with you what I discovered and the daily prayer it led me to pray. You will see how and why I scrapped all the mottoes of self-improvement and self-generated efforts to be better and good by my own strength. Here is how it happened.

One day, years ago, when I was feeling particularly defeated in my efforts to become a better Christian, I read the thirteenth verse of Ephesians 4. Years of study had given me some measure of the "knowledge of the Son of God"—His life, message, death, and resurrection. What eluded me was both an understanding and experience of the "measure of the stature of the fullness of Christ." What did this mean? How could I realize it? That morning, I set a new purpose for my life. Whatever else I achieved, the fullness of Christ would be my primary goal.

THE SEARCH FOR FULLNESS

I ended my quiet time that morning by praying simply, "Lord, I'm tired of struggling to be a better Christian. I long to know and experience the fullness Paul has promised. What is it? Show me the secret of it and I will spend the rest of my life living in it." God's answer to my prayer was greater than I had dared to imagine.

The next weeks of my Bible study focused on the word "fullness." I was reminded that the Greek word *pleroma* means "that which fills or the state of being full." As I searched the New

Testament for passages using the word, I discovered that it was used for what happened in Christ in the Incarnation and what was offered to us through Him.

The apostles John and Paul then became my guides. John writes of the fullness of Christ in the prologue of his gospel: "And the Word became flesh and dwelt among us, and we beheld His glory, the glory as of the only begotten of the Father, *full* of grace and truth. . . . And of His *fullness* we have all received, and grace for grace" (John 1:14, 16, italics added).

Through the Incarnation the fullness of God came to us and was revealed to us. Christ's earthly life displayed the fullness He now offers us.

THE GOD-MAN

In Christ the fundamental union of the divine and human natures mysteriously blended. He was fully human and yet fully divine. Paul puts it clearly, "For it pleased the Father that in Him all the fullness should dwell" and "For in Him dwells all the fullness of the Godhead bodily" (Col. 1:19; 2:9). Nothing was left out! In the Messiah all of the majesty, power, love, and grace of God took on human form. In Christ's brief life we behold fullness. The heart of God is revealed in Christ's character, words, attitudes, mighty deeds, and grace.

At this point in my search for fullness, I had not discovered anything that I had not known or believed before. However, I was beginning to understand the awesome dimensions of the fullness for which I was searching. The life of Christ on earth defined this fullness. The mind of Jesus was filled with God. His emotions were open to the flow of God's Spirit. His body was infused with the radiance of God. He was Emmanuel, God with us.

What, then, did Paul mean by saying we could come to "the measure of the stature of the fullness of Christ"? I pondered his words to the Colossians about "Christ in you, the hope of glory" (Col. 1:27). I vaguely understood these words, but they were not real to me. Christ in me? The fullness of Christ in my mind, emotions, will, and body? Although I had often preached about this, the power of the words had not gripped me personally.

THE SECRET

Then, one day on my pilgrimage, I stumbled on Paul's yearning desire for the Galatians: "My little children, for whom I labor in birth again until Christ is formed in you" (Gal. 4:19). These words became the key. The whole process of realizing the fullness of Christ is like conception, natal formation, birth, growth, and maturity.

Just as Christ was conceived in the Virgin Mary, so too the first step in receiving fullness is for Christ to be conceived and born in us. This means yielding our total self to be the residence of His Spirit. All we can do is say with Mary, "Let it happen, Lord. Be born in me!"

Each Christmas we sing Phillips Brooks's carol "O Little Town of Bethlehem" with thoughtless sentimentality. "O holy Child of Bethlehem, descend to us we pray; cast out our sin and enter in, be born in us today." I've often wondered if we realize what a radical prayer this is. We can pray, "O Christ in all Your fullness, descend to us we pray, cast out our sin and enter in, be born in us today."

Thus begins the dynamic process which goes on all throughout our lives. This process prompts me to pray a daily prayer. For me, this prayer has been the secret of my increasing understanding of the fullness of Christ. I pray it every morning and often throughout the day: "Christ be formed in me!"

A REVERENT CONVICTION

Similarly to Christ's Incarnation, His Spirit dwells in our humanness and He is formed in us. The more we yield our lives to Him, the more He forms us into His image. It is a lifelong process. He's never finished with us. To pray that Christ be formed in us is another way of repeating Mary's words, "Be it done to me according to your word." Whatever of ourselves we yield, Christ fills with Himself.

THE GOAL

The end result of all of this is expressed by John in 1 John 3:2: "When He is revealed, we shall be like Him, for we shall see Him as He is." This time of revelation is not just reserved for Christ's second coming, or when we get to heaven. It also comes in times when He gives us glimpses of what we were and what He has enabled us to become because of His indwelling, transforming work within our minds, emotions, wills, and bodies.

TOO MUCH TO EXPECT?

Is this too much for us to expect? Not if we take seriously Christ's promise to abide in us. And not if we come to grips with Paul's life as well as his admonitions. Christ can be born in us, formed in us, and grow in us as we live each hour.

Have you ever prayed for Christ to be formed in you? I've asked Christians this repeatedly. Over the years, few have answered yes.

Often we think of Christ as outside of us, as being out there somewhere. We pray, hoping for His strength and help in our struggles. We long for His inspiration for our minds and hearts and His intervention in our difficulties. We accept and plead for His power to be released in life around us. But when His fullness pervades us, our perception of the world around us and what He can do changes. He gives us the vision of what He will do and how we are to cooperate with Him.

The fullness of Christ includes His mind for our thoughts, His nature for the formation of our character, His person for the shaping of our personalities, His will for the direction of our wills, and His power for our actions.

POWER TO FACE STRUGGLES

Once we yield our inner lives to the formation of Christ in us, we can face the struggles of our outer lives. Each new challenge or difficulty calls for greater inner growth in His fullness. Our first reaction will not be to cast about for direction or solutions in the circumstances, but to turn to Christ. We can thank Him that out of the fullness of the wisdom, knowledge, and vision of His divine intelligence we will be guided in what to think and what to do. The otherwise disturbing pressures of life will become an occasion for the further formation of Christ's fullness in us. In greater degree, every day we will think and react in oneness with Him.

There is also a direct correlation between our growing knowledge of Christ and our prayer that more of Him be formed in us. Each new discovery of who He is and how He works will be a new step in discovering a greater dimension of His fullness in us. What Jesus said and did on earth continues to be expressed and accomplished in our inner being. We hear the echo of His promises in our minds as He speaks anew in us. We dare to serve others as He works through us, and we become an extension of Christ to them.

LIFE'S THREE BIGGEST STRUGGLES

When we pray that Christ in His fullness be formed in us, we are relieved of three troublesome struggles of life. The first is our struggle with our human nature. It is a long, weary, grim battle to try to change ourselves. Resolutions, improvement programs, and efforts at self-discipline yield little change in our basic nature. But when we honestly confess our defeat in trying to get better and ask for the fullness of Christ, He enters in and performs a continuing miracle of making us like Himself.

Second, we are freed from the struggle to be adequate. I know I am insufficient for the demands of life, but I also know Christ is all-sufficient. I cannot imagine any problem He cannot solve, any person He could not love, and any challenge He would not be able to tackle. And so, from within me, Christ is at work giving me what I could never produce without Him.

Third, we don't have to struggle with worries over what the future holds. What the Lord allows to happen will be used for the greater growth of His fullness in us. We can relax. Whatever we face will be an occasion for new dimensions of His character to be formed in us.

WHAT ABOUT THE CHURCH?

Think for a moment what could happen in the church if we made the fullness of Christ our united quest! So much of our limited vision, lack of love and forgiveness, and unwillingness to serve each other and the world would be transformed.

Paul's challenge that the Christians in Asia Minor press on to the "unity of the faith, knowledge of the Son of God, to a perfect man, to the measure of the stature of the fullness of Christ" was meant for the church as a whole as well as for individual Christians. He envisioned the church as a new humanity filled with the fullness of Christ.

But this can happen only when we yield to this fullness individually. Like any renewal movement, it must begin with one person, lead to a group, and finally end in the congregation as a whole. The fullness Christ offers needs to be preached, taught, modeled, and prayed for today. Instead of guilt-producing sermons on what we "ought" to do and be as Christians, we need to experience and share the secret of Christ's fullness. If we were ever to pray that Christ be formed in us as individuals and as churches, lives would be transformed into Christlikeness, churches would be ablaze with His love and power, and those outside the church would be drawn magnetically to seek the secret of our joy and freedom.

It was thirty years ago that I began praying that Christ be formed in me and that I would receive the fullness of Christ. As I mentioned in an earlier chapter, this was eight years after I had become a Christian and was caught in the mire of trying to live up to the standards of being a Christian. The day that I yielded to the formation was only a beginning. Since then, the transforming process has never stopped. Each day is a new beginning in yielding more of me to the inrush of Christ's fullness.

16

A
NEW
MIND
EVERY
MORNING

One New Year's Eve a good friend grasped my hand and looked me squarely in the eye. Instead of the usual, jolly "Happy New Year!" greeting, he said warmly and thoughtfully, "Lloyd, I pray that this will be the best year of your life."

I thought a lot about that affirming wish during the first days of that year. The best year of my life? What would make it so?

How would you respond? What could make this year one of your best, a year with few problems, good health, and the accomplishment of your hopes and dreams? What year in the past would you consider one of your "best years"?

As I think about this, I am amazed to realize that one of the years in the past I would consider a really "best year" was filled with challenges, difficulties, and trouble. Does this surprise you? It shouldn't. Unless I miss my guess, you probably would agree that a truly great year of your past was one in which you faced and conquered some seemingly insurmountable odds. You were stretched to grow as a person and were stronger because of the mountains of adversity you succeeded in climbing. From the mountain peak you knew that the climb was worth it.

Also, from your new, elevated vantage point you could see new mountains to climb.

Our Best Year

The "best year" of my past was a year in which I made a momentous discovery. The Lord taught me to live in day-tight compartments. The year of my life was made up of great days, each of which I lived to the fullest, as if each were my last. The cumulative result was a year of spiritual power and growth in the midst of concerns which might have rendered it the worst year of my life.

So, in response to my friend's hope that I would have one of the best years of my life, I commit myself to living one day at a time, unreservedly open to the blessings the Lord has prepared.

"Joyous New Day"

If I were to greet you some morning by saying, "Joyous new day!" you might be startled. I don't just mean "Good morning" or "Have a nice day," but "Joyous new day!" This greeting expresses my new outlook. It also expresses my hope for you—that your day would be a new beginning with yesterday's hurts forgiven and all failures forgotten.

It is true that:

> Who bears in mind misfortunes gone
> Will live in fear each hour,
> The joyous person whose heart is right
> Gives no such shadows power.
> He bears in mind no haunting past
> To vex his life on Monday.
> He has no graves within his mind
> To visit every Sunday.

Does it ever happen to you? Do you ever find that you begin a new day bogged down with yesterday's frustrations, fears, or failures? Do you ever get discouraged about unfinished tasks, or have you ever procrastinated about certain projects? Have you ever begun a new day with the feeling, "Oh, well, one more day for a further pile-up of more unfinished tasks"?

Do the challenges of the future ever put a cloud over a new day? Do you often worry so much about what's ahead that you find it difficult to tackle joyously what's at hand? A Scots friend of mine has a wonderful motto: "There are two days about which I dinna fret—yesterday and tomorrow!" That leaves today as our only concern.

JUST FOR TODAY

The more I admit to my own needs and to those of others around me, the more convinced I am that one of the greatest challenges we all have is to be able to pray with Samuel Wilberforce:

> So for tomorrow and its needs
> I do not pray
> But keep me, guide me, love me, Lord,
> Just for today.

Down days have a way of accumulating into discouraging months equaling a dreary year. The problem is that these down days become habitual. We soon expect little from a new day and are not surprised when this is exactly what we get.

It's a shocking realization, but spiritually, nobody is a victim. No one can ruin a day for us without our permission. The one thing we have at our command is our attitude, which is determined by how we deal with what happened yesterday and our level of trust in the Lord for our tomorrows.

As we deal with pressures, difficult people, knotty problems, demanding deadlines, and frustrating situations in any one day, we discover the extent of the effectiveness of our faith. Lofty theories and carefully polished phrases may be fine for theological debates, but what we need is power for the battle of daily living.

THE LAND OF BEGINNING AGAIN

Louisa Fletcher Tarkington expressed our longing for a new day to be a real new beginning:

> I wish that there were some wonderful place
> In the Land of Beginning Again:

143

Where all our mistakes and all our heartaches
And all of our poor selfish grief
Could be dropped like a shabby old coat at the door
And never put on again.

To make each new day a new beginning, we need more than zippy admonitions about self-induced "happy thoughts" and self-generated, self-improvement plans. I would not mock your daily struggles with life with more guilt-producing "oughts." Instead, I want to talk about what the Lord offers and provides to make each day truly a "joyous new day."

RENEWAL OF THE MIND

Paul unlocks the secret of daily renewal in Eph. 4:23: "Be renewed in the spirit of your mind." Our first reaction to this is to feel burdened by one more admonition of something we must do. Renew our mind? That's exactly our dilemma—how can we do this, given our memories of yesterday and our worries of tomorrow?

But closer examination of the Greek text indicates that this is more an offer of a gift than an admonition for us to *do* something. In the present tense, the words mean, "Go on being renewed in the spirit of your mind." This is a continuous, daily renewal. But the words are also in the passive voice, indicating something which is done to us rather than something we accomplish. In other words, it is the risen, reigning Christ who does something in us and to us to renew the spirit of our minds.

THE SPIRIT OF THE MIND

Since this daily, continuous renewal comes as a gift of grace, we can examine what Paul meant by the spirit of the mind. The Bible talks about loving the Lord with our whole being. Moses admonished, "You shall love the Lord your God with all your heart, with all your soul, and with all your might" (Deut. 6:5). Jesus echoed this description with a crucial addition—the mind. He also said, "God is Spirit, and those who worship Him must worship in spirit and truth" (John 4:24). Our spirit, plus our mind, is required for communion with God and thinking His

144

thoughts after Him. So what did Paul mean by "the spirit of the mind"?

Throughout the Bible the mind is the seat of intelligence. Our spirit is the contact point and channel through which we receive the Spirit of Christ into our thinking, our attitude toward life, people, and our outlook on circumstances.

The volitional aspect of our brain may also be implied. We must will to receive the Spirit's inspiration and interpretation in our thoughts. The renewal of the spirit of the mind means that we are to have our thoughts controlled by the Spirit. As the mind is the nerve center for all the responses of the body, so, too, the spirit of the mind is the control center of the mind. We do not naturally desire Christ to be Lord of our thinking. Even after conversion, we lapse back into a desire to run our own lives. This is why only Christ can create in us a new openness to Him.

In Phil. 2:5, Paul says, "Let this mind be in you which was also in Christ Jesus." This can't happen without the renewal of the spirit of the mind. Now consider Rom. 12:1–2 in this light.

> I beseech you therefore, brethren, by the mercies of God, that you present your bodies a living sacrifice, holy, acceptable to God, which is your reasonable service. And do not be conformed to this world, but be transformed by the renewing of your mind, that you may prove what is that good and acceptable and perfect will of God.

It is fascinating to note that the Greek words for "do not be conformed" and "be transformed" are also in the passive. Something is done *to* us. We mustn't let the world conform us to its values, ideas, and attitudes. Instead, we must allow the transforming power of the Spirit to renew our minds. Then we will be able to think, know, and test what is the Lord's good, acceptable, and perfect will.

This is possible because of what happens when we become Christians. Paul's invitation to be renewed in the spirit of our minds is nestled between two affirmations—that the Christians to whom he wrote had put off the old man and had put on the new man.

The renewal of our minds by the Spirit of Christ enables us to claim daily our commitment to Christ and to surrender our old ways of thinking, acting, and responding to life. This is called conversion, which means a new birth, a new beginning.

Christ Himself!

What is this new nature we put on? In Eph. 4:13 Paul describes it as that of "a perfect man, to the measure of the stature of the fullness of Christ." As we discussed previously, the term "fullness" means that with which something is filled or the abundance of the container which is filled.

The process of growing as a Christian is consistently being filled by Christ's Spirit—becoming ever more like Him each day. Whatever happens around us in any one day creates a greater openness to the fullness of Christ in us for the next day. More of our nature is excavated for the infilling of His Spirit.

You may be wondering what all this means for living each day to the fullest as a "joyous new day." Simply, Christ offers us a new mind for each new day! As we begin a new day in quiet commitment to Him, He renews our willingness to be captivated by His mind. Within our mind, He assures us of His forgiveness for our yesterdays.

Without His assurance, we cannot live with freedom and delight, making the most of what comes in any one day. With it, He gives us the precious gifts of wisdom for the problems we must solve, accepting love for the people with whom we must deal, discernment for the decisions we must make, courage for the stands we must take for truth and righteousness, and strength for the endurance we must have to take the physical drain of serving as His disciples.

So, who is in charge of what we think? The spirit of the mind! You! Yes, you and I make a choice very early in every day that either opens or closes the gates of the flow of Christ's Spirit into our brain. This is why a definite period of quiet meditation and prayer determines the day ahead. The most strategic moment in this time is that instant when we willingly surrender ourselves to be invaded by Christ anew. He renews us, making us young and viable again.

Often we miss the adventure of a new day. Recently I asked a friend how he was feeling early one morning.

"I'm not sure yet," he answered. "It's too early to tell. I'm not awake and I'm not even sure that God is up this early."

Ah, but He was. In fact, He had never retired. He is the Lord who never slumbers or sleeps. The night and the day are alike for Him in His constant, consistent, loving care.

New Every Morning

In Lam. 3:21–23, Jeremiah calls us to open our minds at the beginning of each new day:

> This I recall to my mind,
> Therefore I have hope.
> Through the Lord's mercies we are not consumed,
> Because His compassions fail not.
> They are new every morning;
> Great is Your faithfulness.

The prophet had every reason to be discouraged and to greet a new day with despondency. He wrote these words after the fall of Jerusalem at the hands of the Babylonians. His people had been dragged off into exile. Yet, in the midst of his lament over what the rebellious people had done to cause the Lord's judgment, Jeremiah was seized by a magnificent thought. God's mercy had not changed. His faithfulness was not diminished. In fact, His mercies and compassion were offered anew with each dawn for the challenges of each new day.

The awesome thought of indefatigable grace invades our minds. We are called to forget our failures and remember the Lord's goodness. And what better description of Christ's presence with us and in us could we have than the mercies and compassions of God?

Someone's Thinking about You

I believe our thoughts of Him are the result of His prior thought of us. Our thinking of Him and asking Him to guide us through any day is because of His prevenient penetration in the spirit of our minds. Our thinking of Him and our desire to have Him capture and condition our minds are the result of His gracious liberation of our wills. As He grasps our thinking at the beginning of a new day, He reminds us that we are loved, that He has washed away our sins and failures, and that He is ready to help us maximize the day for His glory and our growth in His grace. He will neither leave us nor forsake us wherever we are in the day ahead. His faithfulness will not be judged by a smooth or easy life. He will be with us in the heat of the battle as well as in the delights of life. And in each day begun with this confidence we will be able to trust His divine intelligence for our creative work and difficult decisions, as well as His love and acceptance for others in difficult relationships and encounters.

What is the result of a year of days like this? One of the best years of one's life! More of Christ's fullness—more of His Spirit, mind, character, attitude, and disposition. John expresses the compilation of a life of years like this in 1 John 3:2. At the end of this stage of our eternal life, when we leave behind the bodies in which we've lived here on earth, "we shall be like Him, for we shall see Him as He is." And the company of heaven will sing, "How like Jesus you have become!"

Until then, we are offered grand days and the best years of our life. At the beginning of each of these days, as the Spirit of Christ touches the spirit of our mind, we can begin to live the hours of the day, singing:

> Great is Thy faithfulness, great is Thy faithfulness,
> Morning by morning new mercies I see;
> All I have needed Thy hand hath provided
> Great is Thy faithfulness, Lord, unto me!

So say it to yourself as you begin tomorrow. Sing it to the people you meet. Most of all, claim it and live it. Joyous new day, indeed!

17

WHEN
LIFE
LOSES
ITS
ENJOYMENT

Over the years, Tom and I have shared our delights and difficulties in being fathers.

One day, Tom called to tell me he was in real trouble. His teenage son was resisting or rejecting everything he did for him. Tom was aching about what to do.

"You know, Lloyd," he said with anguish, "for the first time in my life, I think I understand the heart of God. I know what it's like to grieve over someone I love."

Imagine someone about whom you have these two conflicting emotions: great yearning for his or her best, and a sense of frustration over having your efforts to help resisted. Do you have anyone like this in your life? A loved one? A family member? Someone with whom you work? A friend?

When we anguish over difficult people in our lives, we sense how God feels when He sees us rob ourselves of enjoying Him and the gift of life He's given us. By identifying our hurt when people we love turn their backs and reject our overtures of love and care, we can empathize with God's grief for us.

This is the awesome thought Paul startles us with at the end of Ephesians 4, "Do not grieve the Holy Spirit of God, by whom you were sealed for the day of redemption" (v. 30). And what grieves Him? Anything that blocks the free flow of His love and forgiveness. The Spirit's ministry is to remind us that we are cherished, chosen, and called. Sometimes, we deny this by our attitudes and actions. When we do, we grieve God.

"But what about the times when I'm anything but a joy to God, others and myself?" you ask. God, in His mercy, will not let us go until things are right between us and Him and we enjoy Him and life again.

The first step toward this reunion is realizing He cares enough to grieve over us. This theme runs throughout the Bible. Listen to His heart yearning over Israel in Hosea: "When Israel was a child, I loved him, and out of Egypt I called My son. . . . How can I give you up, Ephraim? How can I hand you over, Israel?" (Hos. 11:1, 8).

Or, think of the times Jesus Christ expressed grief. We are told that Christ was grieved over the hardness of people's hearts. And we are profoundly moved by the account of His entry into Jerusalem before the cross. He looked over the Holy City, the defiled temple, the defensive Pharisees and the diffident Sadducees. But He saw something more. He saw what His people were called to be. Where was the joy in the jostling crowd? Where was the peace? Luke captures the grief, "Now as He drew near, He saw the city and *wept* over it" (Luke 19:41, italics added).

Immanuel, God with us, cried!

The Greek word Paul used for "grief" is a very poignant human term to express sorrow.

In Ephesians, Paul urgently pleads with us not to grieve the Holy Spirit of God. His admonition is set in the midst of a list of things we are to do or refuse to do because our minds are renewed by the Holy Spirit. Paul is very specific about what can cloud and eventually clog the flow of the Spirit through our renewed minds.

We've all seen those bumper stickers that say, "One nuclear bomb could ruin your whole day." And we think, "Yeah, and the rest of my life, and this whole continent."

150

Paul enumerates the things that can ruin our day and rob us of a lifetime of enjoying God. So, with just-for-today intentionality, we make a commitment to follow Paul's life-affirming guidelines.

THEY WILL MAKE YOUR DAY

When our minds are renewed by the Spirit, our new personhood adheres to God's "righteousness and true holiness." We make a positive commitment to some solid absolutes.

1. *Absolute honesty.* "Therefore, putting away lying, each one speak truth with his neighbor, for we are members of one another" (Eph. 4:25). Lying can ruin our day. Whenever we shade, manipulate, or speak half of the truth, an alarm signal screeches inside us. We spend untold energy covering up the lie, sometimes with further dissembling. This causes an uneasiness inside us which eventually strains our relationship with others. We become closed and tense. Most important, though, it clogs the flow of the Spirit.

   Speaking of bumper stickers, have you seen the bumper sticker many recovering alcoholics display: "One day at a time"? They know that their commitment to sobriety has to be a daily decision. A total lifetime without another drink may seem impossible, but one great day without alcohol is realizable.

   Likewise, a one-day-at-a-time commitment to absolute honesty in our relationships will add up to weeks and years of freedom from the tension caused by lying at any level. We can't enjoy God or life without truthfulness. When we fail, we need to confess it to the Lord and make restitution with the person to whom we've lied, in the same day, if possible.

2. *Absolute graciousness.* In verse 32, Paul uses the word "tenderhearted" to sum up what our attitude ought to be in all of our relationships. The English translation of the Greek word *charizomenoi* doesn't capture the robust dynamics of this word, which actually means "acting" in grace. We are

to be "kind to one another, tenderhearted, forgiving one another, just as God in Christ also forgave you" (v. 32).

That's not easy. Sometimes people upset us, disappoint us, and make us angry. Are we supposed to keep all these feelings inside of us in an effort to be absolutely gracious? No. In fact, when Paul talks about anger, he says, "'Be angry, and do not sin': do not let the sun go down on your wrath" (v. 26). I think the same is true for disagreements, hurt feelings, and resentments.

To resolve these conflicts we first seek the Lord's grace and guidance. Imagine how He would talk through the problem with the other person.

Then, in His power, go to that person. Reassure him of your love, then gently state how you feel. Do it in a way that will not do irreparable harm to your relationship. When Paul essentially says, "Do not sin: do not let the sun go down on your anger," I think he means, "Don't play God in your judgment, don't back a person into a corner where he feels he can't be forgiven, and don't wait until tomorrow to seek reconciliation or restoration of a right relationship."

As a forgiven saint, offer and receive forgiveness. Again, it'll make your day!

3. *Absolute purity.* Next, Paul talks about keeping the Spirit pure. Often we describe a person as being in "good spirits" to express that he or she has a good disposition on a particular day. Or, we say someone with a rotten disposition is "not in good spirits." Something has gone wrong with his or her spirit.

One of my favorite stories is about an Episcopal priest who began a worship service with the traditional words, "The Lord be with you." He expected the congregation to respond, "And also with you."

But the priest's microphone was not working. He repeated, "The Lord be with you, The Lord be with you," but nothing came through the system. Then, he rapped on the microphone. Suddenly, two disconnected wires clicked back together just as he said, "There's something wrong with this microphone!" His words echoed throughout the building.

"And also with you," came the congregation's response!

Do you sometimes feel like something may be wrong with your spirit? We all feel this way at times. In Eph. 5:3, Paul describes several of the things that disconnect our spirits from the Spirit of the Lord.

Paul begins his list with a Greek word that describes a sour spirit—a bitter, resentful attitude that refuses to be reconciled. Our spirits become polluted with the collected refuse of past hurts, slights, and oversights done by others. We bitterly remember what was said or done to us and work ourselves into a wrathful frenzy. Paul describes this emotion with the word *thumos*, meaning an inward indignation that bursts forth in flash fires of consternation. Our rage incites clamor or quarrelsome arguments in which we shout at each other and say hurtful things. Frequently, in our bitterness, we slander others and assassinate their characters, which produces malice and ill-will within us. All this muck must be cleansed out of our spirits on a daily basis if we want a joyous new day tomorrow.

4. *Absolute integrity with money.* Our attitude toward money can also make or break a day—or a life! Paul says, "Let him who stole steal no longer, but rather let him labor, working with his hands what is good, that he may have something to give him who has need" (v. 28). We have the privilege of earning a wage and glorifying God in the way we spend the money entrusted to us. All that we have belongs to Him. Under His guidance we are to distribute the tithe—the first tenth—for His work through the church, parachurch ministries, and organized efforts to care for the poor and the hungry, as well as our own personal giving to individuals in need. How we spend, save, or invest the other nine-tenths must also be in keeping with our

integrity as saints. Our problem is not stealing from others; it's robbing God (Mal. 3:8)!

What does money have to do with grieving the Spirit? Plenty. He is grieved when either our work or our money becomes our idol. He grieves when we live in luxury and give little or nothing to the poor and hungry. He's concerned when we fence off finances from His Lordship. And He's pained for us when worrying over money becomes a habitual pattern and we forget the riches of our spiritual inheritance.

My friend Frank was an example of this lack of trust about finances. Constantly in debt because of living way beyond his income, he was never free from worrying about money. One day when we talked about his problem, I said, "Frank, God is really grieved over what this worry is doing to you."

"He is? Then why doesn't He give me more so I can get out of debt?" he asked, half laughing.

"I'm sure that He wants to help with this present crisis," I answered. "And some of us who are your friends will be part of His provision. But eventually you're going to have to surrender the management of your money to Him. Ask Him to help you write a budget that's in keeping with your income. Cut out the things you can't afford. And Frank, start tithing *today.*"

"Today?" he grimaced. "How can I do that? I've only got a couple hundred dollars in the bank and haven't paid all the back bills, let alone the current ones."

I told Frank several stories of people who found financial security by starting to tithe when things looked the bleakest. This, plus making the Lord their comptroller, brought them out of their financial tailspin.

Frank was finally convinced. However inept he'd been with money, he did love the Lord and was shocked that God could be grieved over what he was going through. That afternoon when we talked, he made his first step. He wrote a check for a tenth of what little he had in the bank and gave it to our program for feeding the hungry. Then, he committed his compulsive spending to the Lord. Months later he began to enjoy living on a realistic budget. The significant thing is that when Frank trusted the Lord with his financial problems, the rest of his spiritual life took off like a rocket!

IMITATORS OF GOD

If the possibility of grieving God is awesome to us, we are equally moved by what Paul says is the antidote. "Therefore be followers of God as dear children. And walk in love, as Christ also has loved us and given Himself for us as an offering and a sacrifice to God for a sweet smelling aroma" (Eph. 5:1–2).

Instead of living in the grimness of grieving God, we are called to emulate His grace. A daring thought, isn't it? We are also called to be followers. The word for "followers" in the Greek actually means "imitators," *mimetai.* God's self-giving grace is our motivation and Christ's sacrificial love is our model. In response to God's tender mercy and loving care, we commit our total life to Him.

A GRIEF AND GRACE INVENTORY

Now, before we press on to the next section of Ephesians, take a moment to answer these questions:

- How are you grieving God?
- What robs you of enjoying Him and life to the fullest?
- Where are you saying, "No!" to Him in your life, in your relationships, and in social justice?
- Which of the absolutes we've talked about is the most difficult for you to live daily?

Identify your shortcomings. They grieve Him. He wants to heal us. And most of all, He wants us back where we belong— enjoying Him!

18

THE
SEXUALITY
OF
A
SAINT

On his way home from church, a teenage boy met a friend who asked him what the preacher had talked about.

"Sex," the teenager responded laconically.

"Really? What'd he say?" asked his friend.

"Not sure," the boy replied dryly. "I guess he was against it."

How tragic. The only thing the teenager got from the pastor's sermon on sex was that he was down on it. But we can empathize with the pastor. It's a challenge to talk about Christian sexuality without coming across negatively about sex. The reason is that we spend so much time condemning what's wrong in our erotic, sensual, sex-centric society that we have little or no time left to communicate the positive power of enjoying our sexuality as part of enjoying God.

In this chapter on the sexuality of a saint, I want to talk about God's gift of sexuality and then share the rewarding commitment of being a counter-cultural Christian.

In Eph. 5:3–12, Paul gives a clarion call for Christian sexuality. Two phrases leap off the page: "As is fitting for saints . . . rather giving of thanks."

You will remember from chapter two that the term "saint" is used for Christians. The word means holy, that is, belonging to God. A saint is one who is chosen, called, and cherished. Out of love and praise a saint wants to glorify God. Saints are not disembodied spirits, but people with the same physical appetites and needs as anyone else. Nor are saints perfect people without problems. They *are* people living in the last decade of the twentieth century who desire above all else to do things God's way and live to His glory.

I'm convinced that when it comes to sexuality, God's way is the most enjoyable way to live. Let me explain why I think so.

SEXUALITY VS. SENSUALITY

Paul calls us to live as is fitting for saints by giving thanks. Thanksgiving puts everything into perspective. When we thank God for any aspect of life, we immediately acknowledge that it's His gift to us. We also assume responsibility to use the gift in a way pleasing to Him. Sexuality is His gift. Continually thanking Him for it is the creative antidote to sensuality. Now let's be clear about the difference between sexuality and sensuality.

Sexuality is the totality of a man's manliness and a woman's womanliness. It is personality in expression of thought, word and action. It is not simply procreative capacity, genital desire, sexual gratification or the distinctive physiology of the two sexes.

God gave us sexuality not just for the perpetuation of the species, but as an expression of His providence. Sexuality is a dynamic force which enables personality to attain its purpose of existing with and for others. It gives us verve, drive, and the will to be creative. Sexuality is nurtured in infancy and childhood in the bonds of family love. It grows in self-giving, reciprocal relationships with friends of both sexes. More than just a physical drive, sexuality is a profound mystery rooted in the human spirit.

Our sexuality is a delight to behold in both men and women. A human being filled with physical and spiritual beauty is a source of joy to God as much as is a breathtaking sunrise. We are to thank Him for a healthy, attractive body, a charming, warm countenance, and the unique, never-to-be-repeated miracle of personality in another person. God wants us to enjoy being men and women and truly appreciate the sexuality of people of both sexes around us.

Sensuality is just the opposite. It results when we wrench physical sex from total sexuality. Sensuality is treating persons as objects. It is gratification in fantasy or action without a responsible, loving, lasting relationship. Rooted in lust, sensuality leads us to become obsessed with a person's physiology rather than his or her total personality. Likewise, we can grow obsessed with our own bodies as a means of attracting attention and manipulating others. Currently it's difficult not to think this behavior is acceptable in our society.

In our sex-centric society, sexuality has been traded off for sensuality. We are bombarded from all directions with physical sex appeal used to sell everything from soda pop to automobiles. Mass advertising plays on our sex fantasies, fears, and frustrations.

Recently, at Christmastime, a fur company ran a full page ad of a woman wearing nothing but a mink coat and a seductive look on her face. Other than the furrier's name the only words in the ad were, "For a coat like this, I'd give you *anything* for Christmas."

At the same time, television and movies shape our sexual values and behavior. Even in "G" movies, sexual intimacy is portrayed as something that can and should be enjoyed apart from the long-term commitment of monogamous marriage. Other motion pictures, both for television and cinema, often depict sexual intimacy as a recreational pastime without any regard for the ultimate psychological and spiritual welfare of the people involved.

Add to this the eroding eroticism of pornography. Often linked to organized crime syndicates, pornography is now a booming business all over the world. It promotes the worst kind of voyeurism. Hard-core pornography not only divides sex from sexuality, but genitalia from sex.

It is in a sex-drenched world like this that we are called to be counterculture Christians in society. This is as big a challenge for us as it was for the Christians in Asia Minor to whom Paul wrote. It helps us appreciate his call for reverence and gratitude for sexuality as opposed to the self-satisfaction of sensuality. The Ephesians had to contend with the sexual orgies of the Temple of

Diana and fertility cults in other cities in Asia Minor. The Christians didn't just face immorality but lived in a society that had no sexual morality at all.

GOD'S WAY FOR SEXUALITY

Living "as is fitting for saints" meant following God's clear guidelines in His commandments and in Jesus' message. God ordained that physical, sexual intimacy is to be enjoyed in monogamous marriage. Jesus affirmed this and condemned adultery in action and fantasy. In His statement on adultery and lust in the Sermon on the Mount, Jesus was very decisive, "You have heard that it was said to those of old, 'You shall not commit adultery.' But I say to you that whoever looks at a woman to lust for her has already committed adultery with her in his heart" (Matt. 5:27–28). He pressed deep into the inner realm of thoughts, feelings, and motives and shocked his proud listeners by the admonition that adultery of the mind is as serious as adultery in fact. The ancient commandment on adultery had been a bulwark against the disintegration of the family. Now Jesus gave them a bulwark against the disintegration of inner character. Adultery in either action or thought was separating sex from a commitment to care for the whole person throughout the whole duration of life.

Firmly rooting his admonition in God's plan for sexuality, Paul writes, "But fornication and all uncleanness or covetousness, let it not even be named among you." The Greek word for fornication is *porneia*. The word for uncleanness or impurity is *akatharsia*. When combined, they cover the range of any kind of sexual intimacy outside of heterosexual, monogamous marriage. The word "covetousness," both in this context and that of the tenth commandment not to covet, means to desire a person's body for selfish sexual gratification.

No sooner have we absorbed the radical, fundamental implications of this, then Paul goes on to censor our crude jokes, our swearing with sexual language, and our verbal denigration of the sacredness of sexuality. "Neither filthiness, nor foolish talking, nor coarse jesting" are fitting for saints, says the apostle. Then, to drive home the point he has made, he declares with hammer blows, "For this you know, that no fornicator, unclean person, nor

covetous man, who is an idolater, has any inheritance in the kingdom of Christ and God" (Eph. 5:5).

Paul is not talking about a slip or mishap of behavior for
which there is forgiveness when confessed. He's talking about a
consistent pattern of making an idol of any form of sexual intimacy
outside of marriage.

We are challenged to confront a basic problem in our society
and in the church.

It's what I call advocacy, the actual promotion of lifestyles of
physical, sexual intimacy outside of marriage.

For example, advocacy for sexually active homosexuality is
being pressed on the church with great force by one of the
strongest lobbying efforts of our time. The demand is that we
recognize homosexual physical intimacy as a God-planned, God-
ordained sexual lifestyle.

There's a great difference between acceptance of persons
who are homosexual and advocating homosexuality! It is one thing
to communicate grace and hope to persons who discover they have
a homosexual proclivity; it's something else to condone sexual intimacy as approved behavior.

The church is faced with a double standard. Through the
years, it has called single adults to live a celibate life. I'm not talking about a lifelong vow to celibacy, but a commitment to a celibate
life as long as a person remains single. Advocacy for homosexual
sexual intimacy denies this alternative.

The result of this is not only the creation of a contradiction to
the authority of Scripture, but a fallout that's beginning to trouble
single heterosexuals. A woman reacted this way: "I've lived a celibate single life for years as a part of my Christian commitment. If
it's all right for homosexuals to live together in sexual intimacy,
why should I abstain from having intercourse with men?" This
question is being asked with growing intensity in dozens of ways
by single heterosexual men and women.

The answer must be that any kind of physical, sexual intimacy
outside of marriage is not in God's plan.

While we resist advocacy, however, we are called upon to
care for the great number of homosexuals who honestly admit a
sexual confusion, are seeking help, and want to live responsible

161

celibate lives. As part of the church's ministry in this area, heterosexuals need to be healed of the sin of homophobia, the irrational fear and uncontrolled rejection of homosexuals. This is especially true for our ministry to homosexuals suffering from AIDS. Homophobia makes the church a house of judgment and bars from healing grace those who need it so urgently.

If the biblical mandate for physical sexual intimacy only in monogamous heterosexual marriage has not been enough to convince us, the AIDS problem should. AIDS is growing in epidemic proportions among both heterosexual and homosexual men and women. The patterns of human nature are seldom frightened into change, however. As a man was overheard to say, "Don't forget your condoms. You never know these days."

SEXUALITY IN MARRIAGE

Considering a positive view of the sexuality of a saint must also involve concern for sensuality in marriage. There is a danger of sexual intercourse being wrenched from thanksgiving for a mate's total sexuality. The complex needs of the total person can be neglected. Sometimes sex can be a device of control or a means of bartering.

Lust, using a person for selfish gratification, can be expressed in a marriage as well as in a stolen one-night interlude. The problem arises when a person thinks too much of his or her own needs and too little of the other's fulfillment. A husband or wife can be a sex object in marriage with a denigration of his or her own personhood. Sex is so pervasive and so intrinsically connected with every aspect of personality that it cannot be separated from life as a whole without impoverishing the whole marriage. Sex should be a profound deepening of intimacy, not a substitute for it. The gift of physical sexual intimacy is given to two people in marriage to become one in spirit, mind, and body.

A NEW SEXUAL REVOLUTION

What we need today is a new sexual revolution. There was one in the 1920s that took sex off the taboo list for conversation. Subsequently, sex education has taught us a great deal about the physiology of sex but little or nothing about the sacredness of sex. Then, more recently, situational sex was touted as the sure way to un-buckle people's sexual restraints. "What's good is what feels good after" was the motto. Presently, our society is so sex-drenched that both the mystery and wonder of sex are being lost.

I suggest a new revolution. It is to deny the false values of our society and return to the biblical mandates for our sexuality. But instead of a Victorian stiffness, it will be expressed in gratitude and praise to God for the gift of authentic sexuality. We will be able to take delight in the wholeness of the total sexuality of others without an obsession with one aspect of their manhood or woman-hood. Reverence will replace lust. We will be able to enjoy people without misusing them. A new ease and warmth will flow because we know the sacredness of the other person's sexuality. Instead of playing with people as things, we'll play by God's rules and enjoy them as His magnificent miracles.

A young director from the movie industry heard me discuss some of these thoughts about biblical sexuality. He's a new Chris-tian and found much of what I said very different from the world in which he had lived.

"That's revolutionary stuff!" he said.

And so it is. It has been ever since Mount Sinai, the Mount of the Beatitudes, and the cell in Rome from which Paul wrote. The Book of Ephesians has endured through the centuries. The revo-lution it proclaims is the only one that will last. So, saint—enjoy your sexuality. It's God's alternative to sensuality.

with the leaders of our nation or others around the Senate Chambers.

Every day you and I encounter people in trouble—friends with heartaches beneath their polished surfaces, fellow workers who long for someone to care. The Lord has deployed us in our families, workplaces, churches, and communities so we can be used decisively when He wants to communicate His love, forgiveness, and sometimes confrontational truth. I have a friend who begins every day with the prayer, "Lord, make me usable, put me where I can be used, help me be useful so when this day ends, I won't feel useless!"

Buying up the time is something like working on the floor of the stock exchange. Quick decisions must be made under great pressure with many distractions.

We need wisdom and discernment to know what to do or say to make the most of every opportunity. Paul reminds us of our purpose of buying up time—"because the days are evil." Indeed they are. No one needs to convince us of the influence of Satan over people and situations. And since his schemes are so subtle in holding back the forward movement of the kingdom of God, we need daily, hourly guidance and power. No wonder Paul goes on to say, "Therefore do not be unwise, but understand what the will of the Lord is" (v. 17).

The word for "unwise" really means without reason, a reckless and careless pattern of thinking. In other words, Paul says not to try to make the most of every opportunity without consistent patterning by the Lord. We are in a battle with Satan, who does not easily release his grip on people and circumstances we want to win for Christ.

The Lord has a strategy for each situation and relationship. Prolonged time in prayer prepares us for them. Often the Lord shows us beforehand what we are to say and do. Other times, He reveals His will at that moment. We don't need to excuse ourselves from a conversation or meeting for private prayer, for when we open the channel of our minds to the Lord daily, we can expect the fulfillment of Jesus' promise, "Do not worry about how, or what you should answer. For the Holy Spirit will teach you in that very hour what you ought to say" (Luke 12:11). That assurance brings us to Paul's next encouragement for the time of our life.

SPIRIT INTOXICATED

We are to keep on being filled with the Holy Spirit. "And do not be drunk with wine, in which is dissipation; but be filled with the Spirit" (Eph. 5:18).

In Asia Minor, where the cult of Dionysus, the god of wine, was rampant, the Christians were being beguiled with the idea that intoxication with wine was a means to inspiration. Perhaps some of them had been in the cult prior to becoming saints. Instead of intoxication with wine, Paul calls the Christians to "be filled with the Spirit."

The people to whom Paul wrote had been sealed by the Spirit with an initial infilling and had had repeated fresh infillings each new day and for each new challenge.

Note Paul's use of the present passive imperative. Being filled with the Spirit is for now, is done for us rather than by us, and is energetically asked for. "Keep on being filled" is the sense of Paul's admonition. This is the real secret of making the most of every hour and of every opportunity.

From Acts we know that the disciples were filled at Pentecost with the Spirit and had repeated fresh infillings. Just as yesterday's stale grace will not do for today's pressures, so, too, our previous experience of the Spirit's inspiration will not suffice for the new challenges that come to us. Nor can we store up the Spirit as if we were reservoirs or holding tanks for spiritual power to be released at our will. Rather, we are to live daily in the flow of the Spirit's power, gifts, and fruit.

Bill explained how he discovered the hourly filling of the Spirit. "I was one of those Christians who took great pride in my baptism by the Spirit. I loved to talk about the assurances and excitement I felt when the Spirit filled me. But I was living in the past. Now I've realized that was for then, to get me moving. Now to stay moving, I need a new anointing every day . . . and over and over again throughout the day."

The indwelling Spirit makes us wide awake to opportunities and gives us the freedom to enter into the present moment knowing we'll have exactly what we need.

And remember that the indwelling Spirit is Himself the joy we need to enjoy God. So having the time of our life throughout each day is something that happens in us regardless of the grimness of people or circumstances around us.

SING YOUR WAY THROUGH THE DAY

The indefatigable joy of the Spirit enables us to sing our way through the day. Paul suggests that we speak "to one another in psalms and hymns and spiritual songs, singing and making melody in your heart to the Lord" (v. 19).

One of my wife Mary Jane's favorite old movies is *Singing in the Rain*. In fact, she had one of the old posters from the movie framed and hung on the wall of our kitchen. The poster shows Debbie Reynolds, Gene Kelly, and Dennis O'Connor with umbrellas up, splashing through the puddles, and singing with gusto. As a young girl in our church, Debbie became a Christian. A few years ago, while visiting with her in Las Vegas at a church dinner where she sang and I spoke, I renewed my commitment to pray for her.

But the poster for *Singing in the Rain* does more than remind Mary Jane and me of the movie or to pray for Debbie. We are urged to sing in the rain! We frequently experience clouds and rain in pressures and problems, and we need to reaffirm that they cannot diminish the joy of the Spirit.

It's what we sing that makes the difference. Paul recommends spiritual songs, hymns and psalms. There's a wealth of all three to express the song in our hearts. How about, "This is the day the Lord has made, I will rejoice and be glad in it," or "Bless the Lord, oh, my soul and bless His holy name, forget not all His blessings," or "He is Lord, He is Lord, He is risen from the dead and He is Lord," or "In my life, Lord, be glorified"? The resources seem limitless.

I find it helpful to add to my morning devotions a psalm and a hymn or a contemporary spiritual song. One of them is sure to speak to my need and become my theme song for the day. Sometimes we have a repetitive thought that captures our mind for several days. And sometimes it's negative and depressing. Why not replace it with a song of joy that puts hope in our hearts and rhythm in our steps. It will help us claim the next amazing way that Paul suggests for having the time of our lives—all day long.

Thanksgiving Day Every Hour

Thanksgiving really puts things into perspective. Paul encourages "giving thanks always for all things to God the Father in the name of our Lord Jesus Christ" (v. 20).

Thanks always? Yes. Nothing maximizes our delights and minimizes our discouragements like thanksgiving. It is an antidote to any pride we might feel or a medicine for painful problems. When we thank the Lord, we enjoy what He has done for us in obvious blessings and anticipate what He will do when life gets bumpy. As we noted earlier, thanksgiving for our difficulties is really a method of commitment, a trust that the Lord will use everything to draw us into deeper oneness with Him. Thanksgiving brings release from the tension of having to take credit for our accomplishments and produces resolve to move on to discover the growth we'll experience in our adversities. This is no silly palliative, but the source of power!

You and I have been called to redeem the time, to make the most of every opportunity. It's not just Paul's idea, or mine; it's the Lord's plan for enjoying Him. So why not have the time of your life—all the time?

171

20

THE STRENGTH OF SUBMISSION

I was amazed to see not only the difference in their size, but the obvious difference in their personalities. The woman was tall and heavyset and the man was short and wizened. The woman introduced him to me and told me why they had come.

"We are here because we want you to marry us," she said. "I have asked this man to be my husband and he has agreed. Now, he's got something to say to you," she said while poking him. "Now say it," she ordered.

"We don't want any of that love, honor, and obey stuff in the service," he dutifully replied in a thin voice.

"Is that your idea or is it your fiancée's?" I asked.

"Well . . . I think it's both," he replied, clearing his throat nervously.

Now you may have surmised from that opening story that this is going to be a chapter on the need for women to be submissive to their husbands. Half true. It's really a chapter about the strength of submission for both wives and husbands. In fact, as you will see, I think that submission is the secret to all Christian relationships —in the church, in causes, friendships, and the family.

We hear a lot about no-win situations. We all experience more than our share of win-lose relationships in which one person wins with dominance and the other loses by having to be grovelingly subservient. But I think there are win-win relationships in which everyone wins. There's a quality in these relationships that is essential to enjoying people as a vital part of enjoying God. In fact, even that love, honor, and obey "stuff" may be a part of this quality—if *everybody* makes the commitment.

MUTUAL SUBMISSION

The apostle Paul gives us a revolutionary concept in his call for mutual submission, "submitting to one another in the fear of God" (Eph. 5:21). Actually, the original manuscripts had "Christ" instead of "God." That would be in keeping with the authority God has entrusted to the reigning Christ over the church. The word "fear" here does not mean cowering trepidation, but rather awe, wonder, and reverence. He is our Lord, King of our lives, and Master of our discipleship.

Paul suggests that out of reverence for Christ and as a result of the impact of His dynamic love in us, we are to live in a particular manner with each other—first, within the church, and then within the family. How, then, are we to live? Paul instructs us to be mutually submitted and submissive to each other.

Since Paul's words often have been wrenched out of context, there is far too little understanding of what they mean. We must go back to Jesus Christ Himself to understand the true nature of submission.

Paul clarifies this in Philippians 2:

Let this mind be in you which was also in Christ Jesus, who, being in the form of God, did not consider it robbery to be equal with God, but made Himself of no reputation, taking the form of a servant, and coming in the likeness of men. And being found in appearance as a man, He humbled Himself and became obedient to the point of death, even the death of the cross.

(Phil. 2:5–8)

174

During the last days of His life, Jesus Christ exemplified His submission to be a servant in a remarkable, unforgettable way. When He and the disciples arrived at the Upper Room for the last supper, someone was missing. The disciples noticed it first. "Where is the servant?" they asked. "Who will wash our feet so that we can be properly prepared for the Passover feast?" Then Jesus, taking the basin and the towel, did for them what the servant would have done.

Simon Peter protested with astonishment, "You shall never wash my feet!"

Jesus answered, "If I do not wash you, you have no part of Me."

When Jesus finished, He said, "I've given you an example, that you should do as I have done to you."

For the first time, it began to dawn on Peter that to belong to the Servant-Lord was to be a servant.

The revolutionary new quality of life in and through Jesus Christ is that Christians are called to serve Him by serving one another and the world. The essence of submission is to be willing to acknowledge the ultimate value of another person, to listen to him, to receive the Lord through him, and to grow with him. Submission also employs an essential strategy of the kingdom of God, that of an alternating leadership.

The Greek word for submission, *hupotasso,* is a compound of two words: *hupo,* meaning "under," and *tasso,* meaning to arrange, to line up, to accomplish a task. In military terms it means to arrange troops under a leader to march or to work together in battle or on a project.

In Christian submission the leader does not always have to be the same person. With mutual submission, we accept leadership from others and provide it for others. At one point we are the leader; at another point, we are washing the feet of other disciples. "The servant is not greater than his master," said Jesus. The quality of the church is mutual service. We are to will the ultimate good of every person regardless of what it means to us. We must be open to receive what Christ has to give us in and through the fellowship.

The gift of leadership is given by Christ for ministry. I stress this point because it has implications for everything else that we need to learn from this passage. The apostle Paul suggests that a dynamic relationship, the oneness for which Jesus Christ lived and died, begins when both parties to the relationship are committed first and foremost to Him. Together they must work out the implications of His guidance for them. With mutual submission, they entrust leadership to each other in the various areas of life.

Many of us do not like this. We want to assume leadership on an autocratic basis simply because we have a title. For instance, being the pastor of a church gives me absolutely no rights of leadership that I do not earn daily. If I am not a listener, if I am not sensitive, if I do not pray my prayers, read the Scriptures, and allow others to share the process of what we do together, then I deny the biblical principle. I cannot say, "Just do it because I order it." I am a brother in Christ, called and given gifts to share in the leadership of the church.

The same is true for our relationships with one another. We are to submit mutually to each other in order to receive what the Lord has to give in and through us as we are bound together. The Lord speaks through all people: women and men, young and old, rich and poor, laity and clergy, trained and untrained. We are a fellowship in which the Lord has access through all of us as we seek His will and work together.

WHAT ABOUT MARRIAGE AND THE FAMILY?

What does submission mean in terms of marriage and the family? I think that in both of these relationships it is of the utmost importance. However, we need to put what the apostle Paul said about submission in the context of the background out of which he spoke. We must also understand that the position of women and children was radically altered because of the life and ministry of Jesus Christ.

It was unheard of for a rabbi to say, "Let the children come unto to me. Forbid them not, for of such is the kingdom of heaven." Christ's words set in motion a revolution that changed the attitude of the world toward children. He lived in a time when children were not allowed to speak in public, because they were considered insignificant. In the Roman context, a newborn child was laid before the father for judgment. He had the power to decide whether to keep the child as his own or to kill it. Sometimes, inferior children were drowned. Often, children were sold in the marketplace. People who purchased children kept them alive in order to sell them later into the slave market. But Jesus Christ planted a seed to grow in the culture to change the attitude toward children.

Jesus also changed the place of women. It was inconceivable that a rabbi would speak to a woman and treat her as a person rather than as an object. Also, it was unprecedented that any leader, spiritual or otherwise, would have women in his band of followers. It was astonishing that the early church had women as well as men in its leadership. Jesus Christ gave us a profound understanding that with God there are no categories, but people.

It is in this context that the apostle Paul made a radical statement that must have boggled the minds of the Asia Minor Christians who read it. At that time women were playthings for men. Men could divorce their wives with a brief document that needed little explanation. For the apostle Paul to say, "Love your wives as Christ loves the church," was revolutionary.

Paul's words cut across culture with the fine, sharp edge of the truth of God: The misuse of women had to stop.

Paul went further. In Gal. 3:27–28, he wrote, "For as many of you were baptized into Christ have put on Christ. There is neither Jew nor Greek, there is neither slave nor free, there is neither male nor female; for you are all one in Christ Jesus." Here again the revolutionary principle began to grow, radically altering our understanding of people. Jesus Christ, followed by the apostle Paul, lived and preached in a thing-oriented society in which women were objects to be used, not persons to be cherished.

Still, when this passage is interpreted, often the emphasis only is on the submissiveness of women. Women are simply told to be subservient to their husbands. But Paul talks about the husband expressing a cherishing quality of love and commitment to help his wife be all that she is meant to be. He is to be a priest

in his home, enabling his wife to reach her maximum just as Christ did for the church. The secret is not that Christ died for the church in order for the church to love Him, but that He died for the church because He loved it. This is the quality of love of which the apostle Paul is speaking—the giving, self-sacrificing love of a servant who is able to wash other people's feet. In the context of this love, Paul calls women to be submissive to their husbands.

Paul's words about submission have been used by some people to create what they call the chain of command. They write it out elaborately—Christ, husband, wife, kids, dog, and so forth—as if to suggest that if Christ wants to reach the woman, or the woman reach Christ, they both must go through the husband. In the light of the Incarnation, the gospel, and the death of Jesus Christ to liberate us to be people in direct relationship to Him, this idea is absurd. We all have been called to be a part of the priesthood of all believers. Husbands and wives are to be priests to one another—listening, caring, praying, and mediating Christ's love, forgiveness, hope, and guidance to each other.

Mutual submission in marriage means shared leadership. The husband is responsible to instigate and inspire it. That's leadership. In every marriage there's a difference in talents. It would be absurd for a husband not to recognize his wife's talents in a certain area and accept her leadership. For example, my wife is a super manager of finances, organization, and the vital details of running our home. I would be a fool not to accept her leadership. The policy that guides her management is something we set together to achieve Christ's goals for our life.

WHAT ABOUT THE CHILDREN?

Now, what about the challenge of raising children? Simply to have authority because we are parents is not enough. We cannot hope to raise up children to be like Christ by using autocratic methods and imperious rules and regulations. Children can only grow to Christian maturity in an atmosphere of love, caring, and esteem. When that is communicated, parents can exercise their authority

and leadership with strength and decisiveness. Setting guidelines, exercising discipline, and even giving caring punishment will be accepted and followed when a child knows the security of a cherishing affection and affirmation.

Why is it, then, that one of the great Christian psychologists of our time concludes that most young people go off to college lacking self-esteem? Many of them have come out of Christian homes. Their parents, for all of their rules and regulations, have not given their children a level of esteem that motivates them to want to obey and do what is right. Often children are provoked to rebellion because of the absence of the parental leadership which brings humility, sensitivity, affirmation, and self-esteem. Our children need to see in us what it means to be submitted to Christ. Then they need to observe how mutual submission works between their mother and father under the authority of Christ. Neither bland permissiveness nor loveless autocracy will provide a child with the example and experience of authority.

AUTHENTIC AUTHORITY

We are living in a time of history when we need authentic authority. But this authority must be expressed in a biblical, Christ-centered authority.

Most of us resist authority. Growing up, we either had too little of the right kind or too much of the wrong kind. This is why it is so difficult for us to grow in the Christian life. We resist the Lordship of Christ. We give Him part of our lives, thank Him for saving us and for giving us eternal life, but when it gets down to the nitty-gritty of trusting Him day by day, we run our own lives and wonder why we have no power.

A direct interrelationship exists between receiving the power of Christ and submitting to His authority and control. The Christian life is a Christocentric life. There is no sidestepping this issue. Christ is Lord of all, or not at all. Until we accept Him as Lord of all, we are trifling with the Christian faith.

Mahalia Jackson said, "The Lord can make you anything you might want to be if you just put it all in His hands." The great theologian Martin Luther made a similar affirmation:

"Anything that I have held in my own hand has caused suffering and anything that I've placed in His hand has given me freedom and joy." Out of his profound understanding of submission Luther said, "A Christian is the free lord of all and is subject to none; the Christian is the most dutiful servant of all and is subject to everyone."

A RELATIONSHIP INVENTORY

If you are a husband, have you really submitted to the Lordship of Christ in seeking to be like Him? Yes, you are called to express spiritual leadership, but this is not enough. Until you love your wife as much as Christ loved the church, you have no right to assume leadership in your home. If you are not listening and caring, but are establishing rules and regulations as the sole basis of your leadership, you are missing the mark. The Lord has given great skills and spiritual gifts to your wife. If you are open, she will be able to lead you as much as you lead her.

If you are a wife, give your life first to Christ. Trust Him as Lord of your life. Claim that you are a person of equal status in the kingdom of God. You are not inferior. You are not the lesser in gifts or in leadership capacity. You are a Christ-filled person. When you affirm the love and care of Christ coming from your husband, you can entrust your life to the Lord and to him. Together you can think, pray, plan, and make decisions.

For both father and mother, dare to be disciples. Dare to be strong, but within the context of affirmation and encouragement. Do your children know how great they are? Do they sense the affirmation flowing through you that they are a unique, never-to-be-repeated miracle? In this context your guidance and discipline can and will be accepted.

I would like to close this chapter with one of my favorite poems. It is what I pray my children, wife and friends might be able to say. I hope it might be your prayer.

> For me 'twas not the truth you taught
> To you so clear, to me so dim
> But when you came to me you brought a sense of Him.

> And from your eyes He beckons me,
> And from your heart His love is shed
> Till I lose sight of you—and see
> The Christ instead.*

Submit yourself to the Lord and then to others. Lead with tenderness and courage. It's the way to enjoy God in our relationships.

---

* Leslie Weatherhead, *Jesus and Ourselves* (New York: Abingdon-Cokesbury Press, n.d.), 232.

21

WORKING FOR CHRIST ON THE JOB

Most of us will work 160,000 hours during our lifetime. If we take few vacations and work after hours, many of us will work about 200,000 hours. A housewife will work more than 290,000! Work can be either a drudgery or a delight.

As we move on in our discovery of the contemporary relevance of Ephesians, we receive some salient advice from the apostle Paul for both laborers and employers. It helps us to investigate what it means to be a Christian on the job.

Many people have a hard time reconciling their faith with their job. I want to take an in-depth look at how Paul's message relates to this.

In Ephesians, Paul speaks to slaves and to slave owners. At the time in which he lived more than 60 million slaves inhabited the Mediterranean area. Therefore, Paul spoke of the responsibility of slaves to their masters and masters to their slaves. But as he did, he dropped a bombshell into the world which eventually exploded into the emancipation of people from slavery.

Let's now look at Eph. 6:5–9 and see it in the light of what it means for us to work and to employ others. In place of the words "slaves" and "masters," I would like to substitute the terms "employees" and "employers":

> Employees, be obedient to those who are your employers according to the flesh, with fear and trembling, in sincerity of heart, as to Christ; not with eyeservice, as men-pleasers, but as employees of Christ, doing the will of God from the heart, with good will doing service, as to the Lord, and not to men, knowing that whatever good anyone does, he will receive the same from the Lord, whether he is an employee or an employer. And you, employers, do the same things to them, giving up threatening, knowing that your own Master also is in heaven, and there is no partiality with Him.
>
> (*Eph. 6:5–9*)

TRUE OR FALSE

Now I want to make a series of statements and have you answer each of them either true or false.

- The primary purpose of work is to earn a living.
- A person's value is determined on how well he or she succeeds on the job.
- No one really finds his place in the world until he finds the right job.
- The calling of a clergy person is higher than that of a person who works on an assembly line.
- A church is more sacred than the place where you do your daily work.
- What you do on Sunday is more important than what you do during the week.
- At your place of employment, you work primarily for your boss and report to him.

Are these true or false?

An understanding of the biblical truth about life and our true vocation should have guided you to answer "false" to all of these statements. Not a single one of them is true. They are all cultural distortions.

Work can become a false god and the object of our worship. We can spend our whole lives trying to *find* our meaning in our work, rather than *bringing* meaning to our work. Work can be deified. We can become workaholics, seeking to find our self-esteem in the approval of the people with whom or for whom we work.

How do you really feel about your work? When you get up in the morning, do you say, "Praise God, it's a new day and I can go to work"? If not, why not? I once said to a good friend of mine, "You know, I'm really afraid that the church officers are going to discover what fun I'm having working and they'll cut my salary in half!" We don't usually think of enjoying our work as part of enjoying God. Is it wrong to enjoy your work? Or, is it wrong to spend your life working at something that is not enjoyable?

The apostle Paul has given us a salient, powerful truth that cuts right to the core of how to glorify God in our work. He simply states that we are to treat the people with whom or for whom we work as we would treat Christ. To the employers, he says, treat those who work for you as you would treat your true Master in heaven. With this dynamic truth the church began to discover the true vocation of every Christian.

WHAT IS YOUR VOCATION?

When I initially meet people, they usually ask me four basic questions. The first frequently comes up when I am on an airline flight. The person sitting next to me will ask, "What's your vocation?" I try to postpone saying that I am a clergyman for as long as I can, because people then feel awkward. Yet the question, "What is your vocation?" is one of the most important we can ask today.

Vocation means calling. The basic root of the word is "to call." We are called first and foremost to belong to Christ, then to glorify Him and to enjoy Him in everything that we do. In Christ no vocation is greater or more sacred than any other. Yet many Christians believe that if we trust and love God, we must leave our present profession and become a clergyperson. Furthermore, some believe that if they are *truly* called by God and have the touch of the power of the Holy Spirit in their hearts, they will go into the mission field. Aren't these admirable ideas? Well, no. You will not find them in the Bible. The Bible says that to be in Christ is to be in the ministry. Life is not divided into the two categories of sacred and secular.

Too often we think of work as drudgery or of our work place simply as a location where we can earn enough to sustain life. We forget that everything in God's creation is sacred.

I like the way the apostle Paul talks about work in 1 Cor. 10:31: "Whatever you do, do all to the glory of God." Can you say this about what you do? At work? Whatever your employment, be it typing letters, installing handles on automobile doors, filling prescriptions, performing operations, or counseling people as a psychologist, it is sacred. The Scriptures state that all of life belongs to the Lord. Everything we do must be to His glory. Have you ever considered your job as your ministry, as an exciting place where you are given the privilege of working for Christ?

WHAT DO YOU DO FOR A LIVING?

The second question that people ask me is, "What do you do for a living?" They expect me to give them the name of a job. I always respond, "Christ is my life. He is my living." The apostle Paul did not tell the Philippians, "For me to live is to be a tentmaker." He said, "For me to live is Christ." He brought the dignity of Christ's power to working with his hands as a tentmaker as much as he did to the preaching of the gospel.

I once heard of a terrible epitaph engraved on a man's tombstone. "He was born a man. He was reborn a Christian. He died a businessman." How tragic that his family could not have rearranged the epitaph to read, "He was born a man. He was reborn a Christian. He lived as a minister of Jesus Christ in the business realm."

I love to reflect on a fantastic statement made by George McCloud, a leader in the renewal movement in Scotland and throughout Great Britain. "I simply argue that the cross be raised again in the center of the marketplace as well as on the steeple of churches. I want to recover the truth that Jesus was not crucified

186

on an altar between two candlesticks, but on a garbage heap at a crossroads of the world, a cosmopolitan crossroads where they had to describe who He was in Latin, in Greek and in Hebrew, where soldiers gambled and cynics talked in smut."

Christ died in a real world then and occupies a real place in our lives now. He must be at the center of the real issues in our life. The church is simply a place which equips us to handle these issues in our lives as believers in Christ.

What creates the difficult problem in the world of work today is that many of us have been raised to equate our level of self-esteem with our success at work. If we have not succeeded in our work, we believe that we have not succeeded as persons. We search for value in our work. We try to squeeze meaning out of it rather than to find Christ in it. No icon is more tragic than work and the workaholic frenzy to succeed that results from it.

A good friend of mine was an executive in one of the large corporations in America. He had spent his whole life working toward becoming the president of that company. He had done everything he could to position himself. Yet when the time came, someone else was chosen. I will never forget staying up all night with that man and his wife as he paced back and forth, cursing and crying. Finally, by dawn, he was down on his knees. Though he was a Christian, an elder in his Presbyterian church, and a person committed to living out the Christian life, he had to discover that the real lord of his life was that presidency. When he failed to win the position, after spending most of his waking and even some of his nonwaking moments thinking about it, his whole life collapsed. He was a person for whom work had become lord.

My friend's mistake is really no different than that of a man who is overly committed to his work, goes in early, stays late, takes work home and never takes a day off. I know such a man who ended up burning himself out. After a long period in a mental institution, he realized that he could not separate his own identity from his work.

The problem is not limited to men. I am acquainted with a woman who did everything she could to work her way to the top of her corporation. Finally, she became an assistant to the top executive. Beyond this point, there was no place for her to go.

187

"It became boring," she complained. "The competition was over. I got involved in church work because it took away the boredom. I found it to be the source of the real action. And so I took on more and more responsibilities in the church. As I did, I did less and less on my job. Finally, I left my job in order to go to seminary to be trained as a clergyperson. That's what it really means to be a Christian."

How tragic, I thought. Was not the work she had done in that corporation as sacred as the preaching of the gospel that she would be doing in the ministry? The same is true for men.

Often I meet businessmen who tell me, "If I had it to do all over again, Lloyd, I would do what you're doing. I would become a clergyman."

"Why?" I ask.

"Oh, that's where you can really serve the Lord," they answer. What an unbiblical distortion.

What do you do for a living? Christ is your living. Once you commit yourself to Him as the Lord of your life, then He will give you wisdom, strength, discernment, and courage in your work. It does not matter whether you are a housewife or an accountant or a plasterer or a janitor, the Lord will give you what you need to do your job.

WHO IS YOUR BOSS?

"Who is your boss?" is the next question I am asked repeatedly. My frequent response is that I have thousands of bosses, all of them members of my church, most of whom think they are my boss! After we laugh, I ask the same question, "Who's your boss?" Often people reply with the name of the supervisor to whom they report.

Let me affirm that we report to Jesus Christ and serve the people for whom we work on our jobs. Our self-image is to be one of a servant. As a part of our servanthood, we are committed to excellence. Can it be said that you are one of the most indispensable people in your workplace because of what you believe? Does your life in Christ make the quality of your work and your life so desirable that people want to know the reason why?

An elder of my church once shared with me that a man repeatedly came to him complaining about his job. Everything was wrong, including the boss, the working conditions, and the pay. He asked the elder to pray that these things would be changed.

"I'm not going to do that," the elder answered. "Instead, I want you to go to work a half hour early, stay an hour late, and commit yourself to excellence in everything you do and say on your job for the next month."

"But that's not what I'm asking," the man complained. "I want you to get my boss changed. I want you to rearrange the office where I work. I'm not talking about what I ought to do."

The elder dug in his heels. "No," he replied. "First do this experiment and then I'll pray for your working conditions."

The result was that the man's entire attitude was transformed. He became a positive force in correcting many of the things that he had complained about previously.

Would people distinguish you for your excellence? You and I have been called into being cocreators with God. Whatever we do—preaching a message or running a business or raising the next generation—can be done to the glory of God.

"The earth is the Lord's, and all its fullness, the world and those who dwell therein," David says in Ps. 24:1. He owns your office. He owns your lathe. He owns your operating room. And He owns your home. The Lord is Lord of all.

God deploys all of us to a particular place for the purpose of glorifying Him and being available to people. When the Lord is our boss and we serve the people with whom we work, listening and caring, praying and being available to help, then eventually we will have an opportunity to talk about our faith.

I know an executive who has in his office a long list of all the people who work around him. Every morning he prays for them. He's introduced many of them to Christ.

There is a judge whom I love to visit. When I come into his office, I like to look at the indentations in his old carpet. Do you know what caused them? His knees. This man spends hours on his knees, praying for the people with whom he works and praying to make the right decisions. "This is my altar," he says about the spot where he kneels. "After I've knelt here, I go into the courtroom with greater trust and confidence."

What a change there could be in our world if only we began to think of working as if working for the Lord.

Now, I want you to picture your boss. Everyone has a boss, you know. Even if you are the chairman of the board of a large corporation, you have to report to stockholders.

Can you relate to your boss as if he were Jesus Christ? "Oh, but you don't know my boss," you protest. "Let me tell you about him." Yet this is what Paul calls us to do— to work for our employers as if we were working for Christ.

But it also needs to be said that if the purposes of your company or the direction of your boss is contrary to the gospel and what you believe, then you ought to change jobs. Life is too short to spend it working at a place where the Lord has not deployed us. If after prayer, however, you know you are where you should be, then relate to your superiors as if to Christ and work for them knowing that your security, your self-esteem, and your value comes from Him. Then you can work with freedom, joy, and zeal.

WHERE IS YOUR CHURCH?

What is the last question people ask me? "Well then, Lloyd, where is your church?" My church, as is yours, is wherever I go in the community. Our church is not only in the building where we go to be trained and equipped for our ministry, but also in the factory, office building, hospital, or other location where we work. What does it mean to be faithful and obedient to Christ in this place?

Often, in our workplace, we need people with whom we can meet consistently to share our mutual problems and opportunities and to pray for each other. Members of my congregation cluster in hundreds of these groups all over the Los Angeles basin. They meet for breakfast or lunch, in each other's homes and in the office buildings, shops, and movie and television studios of our community. A central question they consider is, "How can I work more effectively for Christ on my job?" Work projects, deadlines, policies, and personality conflicts, as well as goals and the quest for excellence, are discussed and each person is prayed for. At the next meeting they report in and are given fresh encouragement to press on.

The point is, if we accept as our purpose the privilege of enjoying and glorifying God, then it has to include our work. So one last question, "Do you enjoy God at work?"

22

ARMOR
FOR
THE
BATTLE

There's someone who doesn't want you to enjoy God. In fact, he's working day and night to make you think that's an absurd idea. He knows that if you're intent on glorifying and enjoying God, he will lose the possibility of influence over you.

His name is Satan.

Satan has a very clever strategy. He seeks to trip us up by enticing us to think, say, and do the things that are contrary to God's clearly prescribed way of living in Him, and then to make us feel that we are unworthy of His grace.

Sometimes we repeat Dennis the Menace's explanation: "The devil made me do it." Do we realize what we're saying? We're acknowledging that Satan can influence our thoughts that prompt the hurting, destructive, negative things we do. And we're right. He can and does. He wants to keep us locked into a hedonistic kind of enjoyment that keeps us from grace-rooted, joy-oriented enjoyment that's expressed in praise, faithfulness, and obedience to God and His commandments.

Our minds and hearts are the battleground between God and Satan. While we as Christians cannot be possessed, we can be influenced. Satan can play on our unresolved psychological problems and spiritual doubts. He is able to influence us to do the things that make us feel we have finally done that which will make God stop loving us. We feel badly. And he laughs.

We say, "How could I ever have done that?" Or, "That's the one thing I thought I would never do!" Or, "I guess I'm not as far along spiritually as I thought." Self-doubt is followed by self-incrimination and remorse. We are put out of commission for a time.

Is there no hope? Must we continue vacillating? Yes, there is hope. And no, we don't need to remain helpless victims of Satan's influence.

KNOW AND FACE THE ENEMY

Winning any battle requires knowing the enemy together with his strategies, resources, and battle plan. Paul wanted the Christians to know that it is not just human nature which causes life's problems and conflicts. He challenged them to face the manipulator who is the motivator of selfishness, divisiveness, negative thinking, and negative actions.

> Finally, my brethren, be strong in the Lord and in the power of His might. Put on the whole armor of God, that you may be able to stand against the wiles of the devil. For we do not wrestle against flesh and blood, but against principalities, against powers, against the rulers of darkness of this age, against spiritual hosts of wickedness in the heavenly places.
>
> (*Eph. 6:10–12*)

Our biggest battle is not against people. The enemy is not human beings, but demonic beings who can use people. When we give our lives to God and seek to enjoy His grace, we will become targets of the demeaning tactics of Satan. When a church is on the move, experiencing success in what really counts—changed lives and dynamic ministry of the laity in evangelism and mission in the community—watch out. Criticism, competition among leaders, factionalism, and just plain misunderstandings and organizational foul-ups distract from the forward thrust of revival. Or, people become proud of the very programs or buildings or staff that God uses to bring growth and effectiveness. We quickly become defensive of "our way" and lose our freedom to grasp God's new direction for constant renewal.

Satan is delighted when we blame people or groups for divisiveness or debilitating conflict. He wants to remain anonymous so he can continue his diabolical derision undetected. His wiles and schemings are the problem. Paul says—*face the enemy.* But how do we do this?

PUT ON THE WHOLE ARMOR

Paul had observed firsthand the battle armor of the Roman soldiers. He saw how crucial each part was for protection. All six parts became magnificent metaphors for what he knew we need for spiritual warfare.

The apostle wants us to spend time each morning in the Lord's armory to get suited up for the battle. Our thoughts and inclinations can be protected. "Therefore take up the whole armor of God, that you may be able to withstand in the evil day, and having done all, to stand" (Eph. 6:13).

Any day is potentially an evil day. We have decisions to make, people to deal with, work to do, and challenges to meet. What's more, we have temptations to face. We need to put on the whole armor early each day before we meet anyone or attempt anything. The wonderful thing about God's whole armor is that it protects every part of our being. Let's get suited up!

BRACING TRUTH

The first part of the armor we put on is the girdle of truth. "Stand therefore," Paul says, "having girded your waist with truth" (v. 14a). The belt of a Roman soldier's equipment was placed around his waist. It held his tunic in place. Without the belt, his tunic would flap about, interfering with his free movement and possibly tripping him. The belt also served as a brace for the lumbar region. It gave the soldier a sense of strength and stability. That's why Paul associated the brace of truth with standing—"Stand therefore."

Truth helps us to stand with strength as well as to take a

195

stand with courage. Notice that there's no article before truth in Paul's admonition. He's talking about all the implications of truth from Christ the Truth. In Christ we have the ultimate truth about God, His grace and power. We know the truth that Christ died for our sins and that we are elected to be saints. We are loved and forgiven. In the commandments, and in Jesus' teaching, we have the truth spelled out for our daily decisions and living.

What's more, we have Christ's indwelling Spirit to guide us and give us strength to discern and do His will. We have not been left to wander through life with uncertainty. We know what's right and can ferret out falsehood. Jesus said, "If you abide in My word, you are My disciples indeed. And you shall know the truth, and the truth shall make you free" (John 8:31–32).

Abiding in Christ is the way we become braced with His truth. He constantly brings us back to reality—His truth about God, about us, about how life is to be lived, and about the specifics of what obedience to Him entails.

My friend Colin puts it this way. "Knowing Christ sure takes the guesswork out of living. I don't have to spend my energies thrashing about. The basics are so clear and if I'll listen in prayer, the specific marching orders are not long in coming. What a great way to live!"

Satan has a difficult time manipulating a person like Colin because he responds to Satan's tactics and says, "That's just not true and I'll have no part of it." This kind of vigilance with the supporting brace of truth cuts Satan off in his initial efforts to lead us astray.

We are called to love the Lord with our minds, to think clearly about His revealed truth, and to live our lives in congruence with it. Daily Bible study kneads into our minds and souls the truth we need for every situation.

THE BREASTPLATE OF RIGHTEOUSNESS

Closely related to the brace of truth is the breastplate of righteousness. The truth about our righteousness with God by faith in Christ protects us from Satan's scheming efforts to make us insecure. He is the author of the lie that we should try to earn our status with God. The tenet that he's constantly trying to sell is that if we're good enough we can earn God's love, or if we work harder, we'll earn our salvation.

Often we think Satan's influence is limited to ghastly things he tempts us to think or do. No, one of his most effective maneuvers is to encourage self-righteousness. If he can get us into his program of earning our salvation, he has begun to win in his effort to keep us from enjoying grace.

We are called by the Lord to live righteously because we have been made righteous through Christ, not in order to some day measure up. Right behavior follows a right relationship with God.

Susan, a renewed Christian in my church, explained her discovery of righteousness in a powerful way. "For years," she said, "I kept God in the category of a big daddy. I've spent my life trying to please my dad and have never pulled it off. Without realizing it, I projected to God my dad's attitude that I'd be loved more if I always did the right thing. It has been shocking to realize that God's love is not qualified. I am right with Him because of my faith in Christ. And, you know, it makes me want to do what's right. Now I have a motive for morality rather than just a lot of grim 'oughts.' I really want to do what's right because I am right with God." Susan has the breastplate of righteousness.

The breastplate covered a Roman soldier's armor front and back from neck to waist. It was made of layered metal petals intertwined with mail mesh. Some breastplates were made of a single piece of hammered metal shaped to fit closely on the chest. The purpose of the breastplate was to protect the heart and lungs from blows or the piercing penetration of an arrow, sword, or lance.

Our spiritual hearts, or the zone of feelings, need no less protection. Have you ever noticed that you feel emotions in your chest? What we think is directly tied to the pumping of adrenaline that has an immediate impact on how we feel. We talk about heartaches or feeling something in our gut.

·The intellectual knowledge of our righteousness with God plus the gift of faith to accept it has a powerful effect on our emotional stability. Mind you, I am not suggesting that righteousness is only a matter of feeling. What I am saying is that the intellectual comprehension of it directly conditions our emotions.

Christ is our righteousness. He covers us with what Isaiah called the robe of righteousness (Isa. 61:10). Paul wrote the Philippians, "That I may gain Christ and be found in Him, not having my own righteousness, which is from the law (what he could earn) but that which is through faith in Christ (a free gift), the righteousness which is from God by faith" (Phil. 3:7–9, parenthesis added). Having this assurance we are protected from the roller coaster of emotional highs and lows.

Most of all, with the breastplate of righteousness in place, Satan will not be able to influence us with uncertainties about our relationship with God or get us off track by pushing us to strive for what is ours already. And with this security we will be motivated to righteous living. We'll run with the Master with new shoes.

THE PREPARATION OF PEACE

The next aspect of our equipment for battle is our shoes. "Having shod your feet with the preparation of the gospel of peace" (v. 15). The shoes Paul observed on Roman soldiers were half boots called *caliga*. They were made of leather, had open toes, and were tied around the ankles and shins with straps. The soles were thick and heavy and were studded with hobnails.

These shoes had been carefully designed to provide sure-footed stability and to protect the soldier against sharp objects placed in a battlefield. Often an enemy would place in the ground sticks sharpened to dagger points to cripple an advancing legion.

You may wonder what a Roman soldier's shoes have to do with our battle against Satan's influence and particularly how these shoes can be associated with "the preparation of the gospel of peace."

The word "preparation" in Greek is *hetomasia* and denotes readiness or sure-footed foundation. Both shades of meaning probably were in Paul's mind. In the Christian's walk, the unassailable peace of Christ does make us alert and sure-footed in the slippery places. It also protects us from the traps and field spears Satan may have put in our way. The main thing Satan wants to do is put us out of commission. He can't do this when we are protected by peace.

198

Peace is the direct outgrowth of righteousness. Peace with God provides the peace of God. It is the profound assurance of our forgiveness and reconciliation with God through the cross. The estrangement and conflict is over. When this peace grips us, we are compelled to share it with others. We wonder if Paul had Isa. 52:7 in mind, "How beautiful upon the mountains are the feet of him who brings good news, who proclaims peace," when he wrote these verses to the Ephesians. Satan can't harass a person who has peace and whose purpose is to share that peace with others.

A SHIELD AND HELMET

Now Paul tells us about the fourth piece of protective equipment for a soldier-saint, when he writes: "Above all, taking the shield of faith with which you will be able to quench all the fiery darts of the wicked one" (Eph. 6:16). The shield Paul is talking about was called a *scutum* in Latin. It was made with wood-covered linen and leather, with iron strips fastened to the top and bottom. Tall and oblong, the shield protected the whole soldier from the enemy. Its construction was designed to withstand incendiary arrows dipped in pitch and lighted before being sent from the archer's bow.

Most of us can readily understand what's meant by "the fiery darts of the evil one." When our shield of faith is down, we are pierced by flaming arrows that ignite our impatience, anger, or desires. We can flame with indignation, defensiveness, or destructive criticism. Satan's fiery darts can also be sent into our conscience to set a blaze of guilt over unconfessed sins. Other flaming arrows instigate adultery in the mind with all the fiery passions expressed on the picture screen of our fantasies.

How can the shield of faith protect us against these incendiary arrows of Satan? I believe Paul is thinking of the gift of faith that trusts God with our needs moment by moment. A fiery dart can set aflame only the kindling of an unsurrendered need. Intimate, personal, ongoing prayer enables us to trust God with our concerns. And when we see the flaming arrow heading toward us, we can lift our shield and make a fresh commitment to our Lord.

The helmet of salvation is closely related to the shield of faith. It protects our brain, not only from fiery darts but from destructive blows that Satan inflicts to hammer away at our security, stability, and safety—now and for eternity. Our thinking is constantly refortified by the special messages the Lord gives us. This leads us to the sixth part of our weaponry for the battle with Satan.

THE SWORD OF THE SPIRIT

"And take the sword of the Spirit, which is the word of God" (Eph. 6:17). The sword Paul had in mind was a short dagger used in hand-to-hand combat. For close encounters with Satan, we have the power of the Spirit to bring to mind just the right Scripture promise to cut off his attack. The term Paul used for "word" here is *rhema* rather than *logos.* Jesus Christ is the divine *logos,* God's incarnate Word of revelation of Himself. "In the beginning was the Word, and the Word was with God, and the Word was God . . . and the Word became flesh and dwelt among us" (John 1:1, 14). *Rhema,* on the other hand, is used for a saying of the Lord that is particularly applicable to a specific need. The Scriptures are filled with these propitious promises. When we store them up in our minds, the Spirit brings just the right one to mind to claim victory over Satan's influence.

For example, when we are exhausted and need strength, the Spirit uses a *rhema* like Isa. 40:31, "But those who wait on the Lord shall renew their strength; they shall mount up with wings like eagles, they shall run and not be weary, they shall walk and not faint."

Or, when Satan plays on our fears, Isa. 43:1–2 becomes a sword of the Spirit: "Fear not, for I have redeemed you, I have called you by your name; you are Mine. When you pass through the waters, I will be with you; and through the rivers, they shall not overflow you."

Take a hold of Jer. 33:3 as a sword when you feel boxed in on all sides by what seem to be impossibilities. "Call to Me, and I will answer you, and show you great and mighty things, which you do not know."

And what about those times when you try to glorify the Lord in your life and Satan ridicules your confidence that the Lord takes pleasure in your enjoyment of Him? Let the Spirit whisper Jer. 9:23–24 in your soul: "Let not the wise man glory in his wisdom, let not the mighty man glory in his might, let not the rich man glory in his riches; but let him who glories glory in this, that he understands and knows Me, that I am the Lord, exercising lovingkindness, judgment, and righteousness in the earth. *For in these I delight*" (italics added). Or, for good measure, claim Zeph. 3:17, "The Lord your God in your midst, the mighty One will save; He will rejoice over you with gladness, He will quiet you in His love, He will rejoice over you with singing."

That's no fluffy, easy promise. When we hear it in the context of what God had said to His people through Zephaniah, it has an awesome ring. Around 625 B.C. Zephaniah prophesied the judgment of God's people. He speaks God's word of condemnation for unrighteousness, gives warnings and admonitions and then ends with the words of this comforting promise. But it is a promise for those who will accept His judgment and forgiveness. All through the prophecy of Zephaniah, we feel the heart of God yearning for the day when things will be right again with Him and His people. But He knows that will require the cross and atonement. He cannot rejoice over His people, quiet them with His love, and sing over them until after the sins of His people have been cleansed. So, the song of God's enjoyment of us is a post-Calvary, post-Easter reality. Therefore, it makes all the difference on which side of the cross and the empty tomb we are living. When we accept what God has done for us He bursts into song and all the company of heaven joins in the rejoicing. It cost God everything to sing His song over you and me.

When you're discouraged with your own efforts, listen again to Zech. 4:6, "'Not by might nor by power, but by My Spirit,' says the Lord."

Or, when you feel you have to take it all alone, let the Spirit remind you, "For He Himself has said, 'I will never leave you nor forsake you,'" (Heb. 13:5). Or, "Lo, I am with you always" (Matt. 28:20).

In times of temptation, grasp the hope of the Spirit spoken through the apostle John: "He who is in you is greater than he who is in the world" (1 John 4:4); or, through the apostle Paul, "No temptation has overtaken you except such as is common to man; but God is faithful, who will not allow you to be tempted beyond what you are able, but with the temptation will also make the way of escape, that you may be able to bear it" (1 Cor. 10:13); or, through the author of Hebrews speaking of Christ, "For in that He Himself has suffered, being tempted, He is able to aid those who are tempted" (Heb. 2:18).

The treasure chest of words from the Lord or inspired by the Lord seems bottomless. There's a promise for every situation and enough for every day of the rest of our lives.

Some time ago, I gathered promises for every day of the year. I had them printed on cards, put them in a lucite case, and sent them to my friends all over the country. I encouraged them to memorize one a day to enrich their memory bank with hope. Many people took the challenge and memorized a promise a day.

My friend Cary wrote me about the impact of these promises on his life: "I never realized the power of using specific words from the Lord in particular problems. I've been memorizing away as you suggested, and wow, does it ever help! It is as if these Scriptures were spoken just for me. How did the Lord know what I would need? What He says is always on time for the hard times." Cary is discovering how to use the sword of the Spirit.

Prayer in the Battle

Prayer is the way we put on the whole armor of God in the battle. This takes more than a brief morning prayer and a "Good night, Lord," as we're falling asleep. In fact, it requires conversational prayer under the Spirit's guidance throughout the day. He guides us to the word of the Lord repeatedly, hour after hour, and helps us claim a full suit of armor for each situation.

Paul concludes his briefing of the soldier-saints about their armor by reminding them of the power of prayer. Prayer really is a part of our armor. "Praying always with all prayer and supplication in the Spirit." Every moment of every hour on all occasions is to be saturated with prayer. The Spirit seeks to guide our prayers in every challenge and opportunity and especially when the evil one seeks to influence our thinking.

Our great need is for boldness. Paul asked the Christians in Asia Minor to pray that he might be given courage to speak boldly during his imprisonment in Rome, and he knew that they needed boldness as much as he did.

The source of that boldness came from Christ who had defeated Satan. Now, one name sends Satan cowering away with trembling and fear. One name alone can expel his influence and defeat his schemes. It is the name of Jesus Christ.

Claim your authority. Hold out the cross and say, "Stop meddling with Christ's property. I belong to Him. In the name that's above all names, the name of Jesus Christ, you have no power over me or this situation. In His name I intend to glorify and enjoy God!"

23

FOREVER YOURS

A young lad wrote to his beloved, "There is nothing that I am unwilling to do for you. I will ford the broadest, mightiest river. I will climb the highest, most impossible mountain. I will battle the fiercest of beasts. There is nothing I am unwilling to do to express my love for you. Sincerely yours—."

The lad signed his name, thought for a moment, then penned these words: "P.S. I will see you tomorrow if it doesn't rain."

While the statement of what the young man was willing to do for his beloved may amaze us, we are more astonished at his impersonal "sincerely yours" and at the contradictory postscript to his bold affirmations of love.

A businessman once told me, "I sign my letters in three different ways. When it's just a general business letter, I conclude with 'sincerely yours.' When it's a personal letter, I write 'truly yours.' When it's an intimate letter, I just sign it 'yours.'"

The man's correspondence customs made me realize how far the word "sincerely" has drifted from its original meaning.

A woman described to me two young men her daughter was dating. She said, "I must not interfere with my daughter's dating

205

life and tell her what she ought to do, but there's one of the two she ought to marry. One man is sincere, but he's no match for my daughter. The other is bold and handsome. He's the one I've selected!"

Isn't it interesting that she would put down a young man by saying he is sincere? We have lost the meaning of what it means to be sincere.

What does it mean to you? Do you ever sign your notes with "sincerely yours," even when you are uncertain whether you are sincere at all?

In Greek the word for "sincerity" is *aphtharsia,* another expression for something which is continuing, everlasting, indefatigable, and incorruptible. Perhaps we need to think about what we really mean when we write, "Sincerely yours"!

The apostle Paul ended the Ephesian letter by saying, "Grace to all of those who love the Lord Jesus in *sincerity.*" The Revised Standard Version renders it, "Grace be with all who love our Lord Jesus Christ with love undying."

Considering the way this lofty word *aphtharsia* is used throughout the New Testament, it is especially noteworthy that it is used here to describe our relationship with Christ. In Rom. 1:23, Paul uses the word when he speaks of the "glory of the incorruptible God." Then, in 1 Corinthians 15, he employs the word in connection with our resurrection. "The body is sown in corruption, it is raised in incorruption." Similarly, Peter talks about our incorruptible inheritance, and the incorruptible word of God which lives and abides forever, the incorruptible ointment of a gentle and quiet spirit. Note the progression: our incorruptible eternal God has given us an indestructible inheritance so we can glorify and enjoy Him forever.

FOREVER LOVE

So, the words of our living signature are to be "forever yours." What else could a saint say? You and I have been lifted out of the cycle of defeat and decay to a life of dedication and delight. God's love will never change. His faithfulness is sure for now and eternity. And out of our thankful hearts comes our response, "Lord, I am Yours forever!"

206

When Christ takes up residence in us, we become His letter of hope to the world. Paul focused the calling of the Corinthians by this compelling image. "You are manifestly an epistle of Christ . . . written not with ink but by the Spirit of the living God . . . and we have such trust through Christ toward God . . . who also made us sufficient as ministers of the new covenant" (2 Cor. 3:3, 4, 6).

Now there's a liberating self-image: we are a letter written by the Lord to the world saying, "Here's a person who has received My grace and whose joy is an evidence of what it means to enjoy Me and eternal life. I'm forever Yours, God."

WHO DELIVERS A LETTER?

Tychicus was that kind of letter from the Lord. He was in prison with Paul and was probably the scribe to whom Paul dictated the Ephesian epistle. In Acts 20:4, Luke describes Tychicus as an "Asian," one from Asia Minor.

Paul's analysis of Tychicus' qualities is more personal. We are sure that the apostle smiled warmly at his beloved friend and scribe as he dictated these affirming words for him to write: "Tychicus, a beloved brother and faithful minister in the Lord, will make all things known to you; whom I have sent to you for this very purpose . . . that he may comfort your hearts" (Eph. 6:21–22).

What a magnificent, dossier statement about a disciple! Christ in Tychicus had made him a beloved brother, a loving and lovable person. I imagine that he exuded his enjoyment of God. And it's obvious Paul enjoyed him. How many people can say this about us?

But Tychicus was also a faithful minister. The word "minister" is *diakonos* in Greek, meaning a servant. This is our calling as we enjoy the Lord. Our joy and gratitude spill over in serving Him by serving people. Tychicus was distinguished by faithfulness in his service to Paul, the church in Asia Minor, and in spreading the gospel. There's no greater satisfaction in life than giving ourselves to others—with enjoyment.

My fellow pastor, Jack Loo, is one of the most winsome, life-affirming encouragers I know. Often he ends our conversations with some delightful words. Whether we've talked about a personal need, church programs, or some small administrative detail, Jack smiles broadly and says, "It's a joy to serve the Lord and you!" No wonder I'm one of thousands of people who enjoy this Estonian saint, Jack Loo!

Paul told the Christians in Asia Minor that Tychicus would comfort their hearts. The believers were deeply concerned about the apostle in his imprisonment and longed for word about him. Tychicus could be counted on not only to quiet their anxieties about Paul, but to bring them the comfort of Christ. As the Revised Standard Version puts Paul's words, "Tychicus will encourage your hearts." A servant is a comforting encourager who draws alongside people to listen and to help lift their burdens. God has equipped us for the ministry of comforting others.

THE DEMAS DRIFT

By contrast to Tychicus, we look at another of Paul's friends. His name was Demas. He is not mentioned in Ephesians. We wonder if Paul saw in him the signs of his defection from discipleship. The letter of his life did not express a "forever yours" quality of staying power.

It's possible to slide away from Christ and His plan for us for His best in every area and in all our relationships. When we do we are caught in what I call "the Demas drift." But who is Demas?

The New Testament is very honest about the characters in the drama of the early church. It exposes the weaknesses as well as the strengths of the heroines and heroes of the faith. It also tells us about some who didn't make it, people who had a glorious beginning and a tragic end. Demas was one of those. We know very little about him, except what Paul tells us in three different references.

During Paul's first imprisonment, he wrote to Philemon and referred to Demas in verse 24 in the phrase, "as do Mark, Aristarchus, Demas, Luke, my fellow laborers." In Col. 4:14, the apostle's enthusiasm has dampened. Demas is mentioned, but without commendation or affirmation: "Luke the beloved physician and Demas greet you." Then, in 2 Tim. 4:10, Paul is more forthright: "for Demas has forsaken me, having loved this present world."

Note the drift: Demas, my fellow laborer; Demas; Demas has forsaken me. Demus lacked *aphtharsia.*

You and I have been programmed for growth in *aphtharsia:* undying, forever love for Christ and others. We ask ourselves: Are we closer to being a "forever yours" saint today than we were a year ago? Are our relationships with others deeper, more caring and loving?

What about our impact on the world around us? Are we involved now in serving people and in confronting and changing that which debilitates and dehumanizes people? Most of all, is our relationship with the Lord more vital, committed, empowered, and exciting than ever before?

The Demas drift happens when we lose our enthusiasm for what the Lord has prepared for us. The letter people read from our lives would have to be signed, "very casually yours."

I, for one, want my life to be an epistle like that of Tychicus, not Demas. A new paragraph in this epistle is being written today. My prayer is, "Lord, make today's paragraph of my enjoyment of You even more exciting than yesterday's. Thanks for creating me to know, love, serve, *and* enjoy You. And, the wonder of it all, thanks for the privilege of knowing that through all the ups and downs of life, in spite of everything, I belong to You and can bring You enjoyment. That's the joy of my life. Because of Your unchanging grace, I am forever yours!"

How will you sign your life today and at the end of this brief portion of eternity?

LLOYD
OGILVIE
PRODUCTS

Ask Him Anything	tp ISBN 084-9929-822
The Bush Is Still Burning	tp ISBN 084-9930-316
The Communicator's Commentary NT Vol. 5—Acts	hc ISBN 084-9901-588
Congratulations! God Believes in You	tp ISBN 084-9929-946
Drumbeat of Love	tp ISBN 084-9928-958
A Future and a Hope	hc ISBN 084-9906-377
If God Cares, Why Do I Still Have Problems?	hc ISBN 084-9904-544
Understanding the Hard Sayings of Jesus (formerly "The Other Jesus")	tp ISBN 084-9931-363
When God First Thought of You: The Full Measure of Love as Found in 1, 2, 3 John	tp ISBN 084-9929-458
12 Steps to Living Without Fear	hc ISBN 084-9906-13X lpp ISBN 084-9931-401 ac SPCN 201-0521-005
Making Stress Work for You	tp ISBN 084-9930-391 ac SPCN 201-0501-004
Surviving in the Midst of Worry and Stress	vc SPCN 801-1001-795

ac	audio cassette	**hc**	hardcover book	**vc**	video cassette
lpp	large print edition	**tp**	trade paper book		